HIDDEN
HISTORY
of
CIVIL WAR
CHARLESTON

Margaret Middleton Rivers Eastman

THE
History
PRESS

Published by The History Press
Charleston, SC 29403
www.historypress.net

Cover: Hand-tinted photograph of the bombardment of Fort Sumter on April 12, 1861.
Courtesy Charleston Museum, Charleston, South Carolina.

First published 2012

Manufactured in the United States

ISBN 978.1.60949.574.9

Library of Congress CIP data applied for.

Dedicated to my family with much love

Contents

"Photographs of the Federal Navy, and seaborne expeditions against
the Atlantic Coast of the Confederacy, specifically of Charleston, S.C.
1863-1865. General Gillmore's success at Fort Pulaski earned him
the conduct of a much more difficult undertaking: the reduction of
the defenses of Charleston Harbor, with the aid of a squadron under
Rear Adm. John A. Dahlgren. Operations began early in July 1863;
by October hard work and heavy losses had reduced Fort Wagner
and Battery Gregg (renamed Fort Putnam by the Federals) on Morris
Island, and had silenced Fort Sumter. But no further progress was
made until February 18, 1865, when Gen. William T. Sherman's
approach overland brought about the evacuation of Charleston. The
photographers who came to record the flag-raising ceremony at Fort
Sumter on April 14, 1865, just 4 years after the surrender with which
the Civil War opened, thoroughly documented the forts, Federal and
Confederate, and the lovely old city, which fortunately had received only
limited damage." *Library of Congress.*

Appreciation

My son, Robert Eastman, who has acted as my literary agent.

My grandmother, Margaret Simons Middleton, a published historian, who recorded the Middleton family history.

Dorothy Middleton Anderson, who published Charles Francis Middleton's letters in the *Bermuda Quarterly*.

Philip A. Middleton, a history buff in his own right, who first provided a story about the blockade runner *Lelia* and verified recollections of family traditions.

Edward FitzSimons Good, for full access to his grandmother's research now housed at the College of Charleston Special Collections Library.

Charles Witte Waring III, executive director of the *Charleston Mercury*, for invaluable assistance.

Amelia P. Cathcart and Paul Cathcart for providing the heroic acts of CSA Lieutenant Colonel William Richard Cathcart, South Carolina Militia.

James Delgado, distinguished author and maritime archeologist, for sharing his research about the *Mary Celestia*.

Richard Harris and Robert Thorpe for contributing information about the Miller family, Liverpool shipbuilding and the blockade runners *Mary Celestia* and *Lelia*.

Chris Michael, author of *Lelia*, for clarifications on the ship's history.

Robert and Suzanne Miller for sleuthing the Crenshaw brothers while on vacation in Richmond.

Ethel Nepveux for information about George Alfred Trenholm and his maritime empire.

Marguerite Palmer and Jack Simmons for their research on Amarinthia Yates Snowden.

Marie Ferrara, Claire Fund, Anne Bennett, Harlan Green, Angela Flenner, Deborah Larsen, Sam Stewart and John White at the College of Charleston Special Collections Library, who have provided a repository for my research and assisted in too many ways to count.

The delightful gang at The History Press: Jessica Berzon, Katie Parry, Daniel Watson, Adam Ferrell, Darcy Mahan, Sophia Russell and Natasha Walsh.

Carl Borick, assistant director; Jennifer Scheetz, archivist; and Jan Hiester, registrar, of the Charleston Museum for continued assistance.

To those who helped along the way: Wayne Braverman, Michael D. Coker, Beth Dickson, Richard Donohoe, Chet Hearn, Robert H. Lockwood, Cheryl (CC) Paul, Robert Salvo and Robert Stockton.

CHAPTER I

The Election of 1860

By 1860, the Union was in a grave state of political unrest. Proslavery and antislavery factions had been at odds for decades, and emotions ran high across the land. In addition, the alignment of the major political parties had changed. Although the Democratic Party still dominated national politics, there was virtually no opposition from the once-influential Whig Party, which had been founded in 1830 to counter the policies of President Andrew Jackson.

During its heyday, Whig Party membership had included Henry Clay, Daniel Webster, Abraham Lincoln and Horace Greely, editor of the *New York Tribune*. Two Whig candidates were elected president: William Henry Harrison and Zachary Taylor. Both Whig presidents died while in office, and neither vice president who succeeded them as president was reelected. The Whig Party met its demise in the mid-1850s due to internal disagreements over slavery and the rights of slave owners in the territories. The political vacuum was filled by the new Republican Party, founded in 1854 in opposition to the Kansas-Nebraska Act, which repealed the Missouri Compromise that had kept slavery out of Kansas.

Another group that surfaced during the 1850s was a radical group of proslavery secessionists. The group's politics had been influenced by John C. Calhoun, whose oratory on nullification and states' rights had helped create in the Southern psyche a disregard for a strong central government. Called "fire-eaters" by Northerners, these radicals urged Southern states to create a separate nation that would protect slavery and their way of

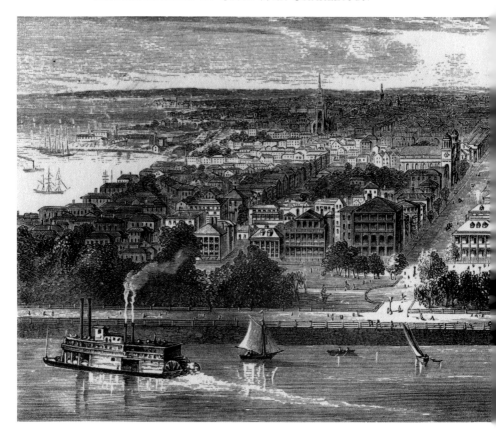

life. Fearing a shift in the national balance of power as waves of new immigrants arrived from Europe, their oratory became more impassioned as the decade progressed. Better-known fire-eaters were: South Carolinians Robert Barnwell Rhett and his son Robert Barnwell Rhett Jr.; Louis T. Wigfall, originally from Edgefield, South Carolina, who had moved to Texas in 1848; the silver-tongued orator from Alabama, William Lowndes Yancey, a descendant of the South Carolina Lowndes; and Edmund Ruffin, a Virginian who is sometimes erroneously credited with firing the first shot of the war.

Splitting the Democratic Party

The election of 1860 got off to a bad start. To placate Southerners after their candidate lost the nomination at the 1856 convention, Northern Democrats had selected Charleston, South Carolina, for their national convention. Initially, it seemed a good choice. Charleston was an urbane port town with a population of forty-three thousand. It was also simmering with sectionalism, difficult to get to and the local hostelries were incapable of accommodating the enormous influx of delegates that arrived by sea, coach and train.

The delegates began arriving on April 18. Those from New York, Pennsylvania and Massachusetts came on chartered steamboats that provided their food and sleeping accommodations. Those who journeyed by

"The steamship *S.R. Spaulding* in which the New England Delegation lives at Charleston." (*Harper's Weekly*, April 28, 1860.) *Courtesy Charleston Museum, Charleston, South Carolina.*

Opposite top:"The Charleston Convention—interior of Douglas's headquarters, Hibernia (*sic*) Hall, Charleston, S.C." (*Frank Leslie's Illustrated*, May 5, 1860.) *Courtesy Charleston Museum, Charleston, South Carolina.*

Opposite bottom: "The Charleston Convention—view of the South Carolina Institute building, in Meeting Street, Charleston, S.C., where the Democratic Convention will hold its meeting during the present month of April." (*Frank Leslie's Illustrated*, April 14, 1860.) *Courtesy Charleston Museum, Charleston, South Carolina.*

rail from Washington had to switch trains six times, dragging their baggage with them as they transferred from one set of tracks to another when the gauge changed. The spring weather had been chilly, and the delegates who left Washington were dressed in heavy woolen clothing. It was unfortunate that it was unseasonably hot and humid when the exhausted travelers finally reached Charleston.

The convention frontrunner was Illinois senator Stephen A. Douglas, who did not support slavery enough for the Southern mindset. (He was known for his participation in the Lincoln-Douglas debates.) Douglas delegates stayed at the Mills House on Meeting Street; over a hundred of his less-affluent delegates bunked down the street in his campaign headquarters at the Hibernian Hall. All delegates touted their candidate, whom they assumed would win the nomination.

Radical secessionist delegates stayed at the Charleston Hotel on Meeting Street, while supporters of James Buchanan lodged at a luxury hotel on King Street. All hotels had raised their rates, and the visitors were further put upon by con artists who flocked to the city to fleece the conventioneers. Delegates with proper social credentials were invited to stay in private homes and enjoyed the very best Charleston had to offer.

The delegates convened on April 23 at Institute Hall on Meeting Street. A kind Providence dropped an icy rain on the stifling city as the delegates walked down Meeting Street. The men arrived drenched and discovered that the cooling rain did little to alleviate the oppressive heat once three thousand people crowded into the airless building.

Physical discomfort and behind-the-scenes intrigues quickly transformed the meeting into the most divisive convention in the nation's history. The delegates agreed to vote on their platform before nominating a candidate—a fatal decision that eventually doomed the Democratic Party's chances for the presidency.

Moderate Southern delegates did not want to destroy the Union or the Democratic Party, but emotions ran high over the issue of slavery in the territories. Having local enthusiasts hiss and boo from the balcony added spice to the highly charged debates. Only Greenville's staunch Unionist delegate, Benjamin Franklin Perry, withstood the unrelenting social pressure of the secessionists and made a speech defending the Union.

Despite Perry's remarks, the convention became so contentious that fifty delegates from eight "Cotton South" states withdrew and gathered at St. Andrew's Hall on Broad Street, where they waited in vain for conciliatory overtures from their colleagues at Institute Hall.

Those who remained at Institute Hall voted, and voted, and voted but could not reach the required two-thirds majority to select a candidate. On May 3, after casting the fifty-seventh ballot, the delegates finally agreed to meet again in Baltimore in June. Before they adjourned, the assembly requested that the Lower South states fill the fifty vacancies before they met again.

A week before the Democratic Convention, Lower South Democratic delegates gathered in Richmond, Virginia, to choose delegates. Although Robert Barnwell Rhett and other radical South Carolinians vainly attempted to sabotage the Richmond convention, in the end, the dissenting delegates from Institute Hall were chosen to proceed to Baltimore.

The National Democratic Convention reconvened at the Front Street Theatre on June 18. This time, 110 Southern delegates walked out over the question of seating delegates who had bolted in Charleston. The remaining Democratic delegates selected Stephen Douglas as their presidential candidate.[1]

Dissident Southern Democrats met at the Maryland Institute in Baltimore and selected sitting Vice President John C. Breckenridge as their candidate. Die-hard Southern Whigs who supported neither party formed the Constitutional Union Party and entered the fray by advocating compromise to save the Union. Their candidate was U.S. Senator John Bell from Tennessee.

In May, the Republican Party met in Chicago and nominated Abraham Lincoln on the third ballot. Representing expansionists and Northern interests, its platform stated that slavery would not be allowed in the new territories and promised protective tariffs for industry, an act granting free farmland to Western settlers and funding of a transcontinental railroad, all unpopular measures in the agrarian South.

In South Carolina, radical secessionists warned that if the Republicans won the 1860 election, the state would have to use its Constitutional right to immediately withdraw from the Union. This drastic oratory was not supported by more moderate heads.

CONSPIRACY

In October 1860, South Carolina's governor was William Henry Gist. After his father's death, Gist's uncle had become his guardian. This uncle was a passionate states' rights champion who had named his own son States Rights. Adopting his uncle's views, Gist made a reputation for himself as a states' rights advocate and long-time justifier of secession. He openly opposed Lincoln's election and secretly wrote letters from Rose Hill plantation to the governors of North Carolina, Georgia, Florida, Alabama, Mississippi and Louisiana to inquire if those states would join South Carolina in leaving the Union if Lincoln were elected president. The governors of Mississippi and Florida replied that their states would follow South Carolina's lead; the others were noncommittal.

Firebrand Robert Barnwell Rhett Jr. also wrote secret inquiries to Jefferson Davis and other Cotton South leaders asking if they would secede. They, too, were not encouraging.

About the same time, Alfred Proctor Aldrich,[2] a prominent member of the South Carolina legislature and a friend and protégé of United States senator James Henry Hammond, requested his opinion about Separate

State Secession. Hammond was a controversial politician who had served in the state house and had been governor of South Carolina. An outspoken defender of slavery and states' rights, Hammond had been asked to fill John C. Calhoun's Senate seat. Although he popularized the phrase "Cotton is King" in an 1858 Senate speech, Hammond had become convinced that most Southerners had no desire to leave the Union as long as their rights were protected. Feeling that Southern obstinacy played into the hands of abolitionists, he gradually abandoned his secessionist views and urged Southerners to make concessions.

It was becoming increasingly obvious that the majority of Southern leaders preferred to wait and see what Lincoln would do before calling for disunion. Wanting to protect their privileged way of life, some Charleston elitists decided to take matters into their own hands. Enter the 1860 Association. Even today, their revolutionary activities rarely appear in history books.

The 1860 Association's members were the very cream of society, welcomed in all the best drawing rooms. Its organizer was Robert Newman Gourdin,[3] of Gourdin, Mathiesen and Company. With offices in Charleston and Savannah, his firm specialized in marketing Sea Island cotton, a uniquely silky fiber that produced fortunes by selling it to Belgian and French lace makers. Gourdin had grown up on Buck Hall, a plantation in St. Johns Parish. He was admitted to the bar in 1834 and was active in civic affairs. Gourdin and his bachelor brother Henry, the senior partner in the prosperous firm, resided in a handsome South Battery mansion that soon became the center of a massive propaganda campaign designed to push the moderate Southern majority into secession.

Starting in September 1860, every Thursday night more than a dozen conspirators met at the Gourdins', where they dined and strategized. Among the distinguished company were its president, William Dennison Porter, an attorney who served in the South Carolina House of Representatives from 1840 to 1848 and the South Carolina Senate from 1848 to 1865; the secretary-treasurer Isaac William Hayne, was then attorney general of South Carolina (1848–68); and federal judge Andrew Gordon Magrath, who had acquired most of his legal training under Charleston's staunch Unionist judge James L. Petigru.

The 1860 Association disseminated over two hundred thousand doomsday pamphlets written by a Princeton graduate, the dapper John Townsend. An aristocrat with all the right credentials, Townsend's country seat was Bleak Hall, the largest plantation on Edisto Island, with 3,779 acres, including marshland. Under Townsend's meticulous care, the plantation was famous for its prize-winning cotton. Townsend attempted to fan the flames of Southern paranoia by declaring that submission meant ruin and would only postpone the inevitable demise of the Southern way of life through the Republicans' use of patronage and federal jobs to dilute the South's stance on slavery.

The Gourdin brothers secretly corresponded with like-minded Southern leaders, hoping to get assurances that their states would follow if South Carolina dared secession alone.[1]

And the would-be Separate State Secessionists had a good chance of prevailing. Because of its archaic form of government, South Carolina was the only state in the Union where legislators had the prerogative of meeting the day before a general election to select presidential electors. The legislature met on November 5 and unanimously chose Vice President John Breckenridge. In case Lincoln won, Governor Gist asked the legislators to remain in session until the election results were published.

Although Lincoln received slightly less than 40 percent of the popular vote on November 6, the Republican Party received enough electoral votes to elect him president, and the stage was set for the disaster yet to come.

CHAPTER 2

Charleston

Day After the Election

The chain of events that led to war began almost immediately. Once Lincoln's election was confirmed, a far-reaching drama played out in the Federal Court at 23 Chalmers Street where Robert Gourdin, organizer of the 1860 Association, just happened to be the foreman of a grand jury. When Judge Andrew Magrath asked Gourdin to deliver the grand jury's presentments, he replied that the federal grand jury could not proceed and declared that the "ballot-box of yesterday" ended federal jurisdiction in South Carolina.

Given the probable secession of the state, Judge Magrath replied that he must "prepare to obey its wishes," proclaiming:

> *That preparation is made by the resignation of the office I have held. For the last time I have, as a Judge of the United States, administered the laws of the United States, within the limits of the State of South Carolina. While thus acting in obedience to a sense of duty, I cannot be indifferent to the emotions it must produce. That department of Government which, I believe, has best maintained its integrity and preserved its purity, has been suspended. So far as I am concerned, the Temple of Justice, raised under the Constitution of the United States, is now closed. If it shall be never again opened, I thank God that its doors have been closed before its altar has been desecrated with sacrifices to tyranny.*

Honorable Judge Magrath. (*Harper's Weekly*, January 19, 1861.) *Courtesy Charleston Museum, Charleston, South Carolina.*

Charleston Arsenal entrance. *Courtesy Charleston Museum, Charleston, South Carolina.*

Charleston: Day After the Election

Whereupon, he removed his judicial robe and stepped down.

Shortly thereafter, William F. Colcock, U.S. collector of the port of Charleston's custom duties; James Conner, U.S. district attorney; and Daniel Heyward Hamilton, U.S. marshal, resigned their federal posts. Only Alfred Huger bravely remained postmaster general amid the scorn of his peers.[5]

The drama that day continued when Governor Gist ordered the immediate takeover of the Charleston Arsenal under the pretext of guarding it against a possible slave insurrection.

According to Thomas Pickney Lowndes:

> On the morning of the 7th of November, 1860, I was informed by Corporal Finley of my squad, that I was detailed as one of twenty picked men to capture the Charleston Arsenal. Not feeling particularly warlike at that time, and fully believing what our leaders told us, that there would be no war because it was unconstitutional, and that it would be a merely a peaceable secession, I suggested that it might be taken as an overt act, and might lead to unpleasant consequences; besides, I had a engagement to walk with a young lady that afternoon, and it would be awkward for me to get off, and begged to get the Captain to pick over. But my appeals were in vain. "Duty," said the Corporal, "calls you to do or die," and I did. Rushing to my friends I informed them of the compliment paid to my desperate courage, and my soldierly qualities. I borrowed from them everything they had in the way of weapons, and a pocket-flask. I was presented with a beautiful scarf as a tribute from "virtue to valor" by the "girl I left behind me," and by my mother with an umbrella, in case of rain—for the night looked threatening. Then bidding farewell to my sisters, and my cousins, and my aunts, who were not as much distressed as I thought they should be under the circumstances, I buckled on my armor, composed of three large and one small revolver, State rifle, bowie-knife, and bayonet, over the majestic uniform of the Washington Light Infantry...
>
> Thus dressed to kill I repaired to the rendezvous, Mr. Porter's church, Ashley Street, stopping on the way two or three times to bid good-by, and realize that drinking is the "soldier's pleasure." There we met under the pale light of the moon a little before the last bell rang. Never shall I forget the solemnity of the scene; the awful stillness so unlike a Fourth of July parade; the church—the place for a graveyard, perhaps for us—no music, no toasts, no health-drinking, nothing but the suppressed breathing of the twenty picked men as they sat upon Mr. Porter's church doorsteps, waiting for the order, "Fall in." Soon this was given, "according to height." Now

this amendment put me uncomfortably near the front line, so I moved that we go "left in front," if I could not be left behind. This motion, with a few very appropriate remarks by the tallest man of the picked twenty, was feeling put by the Lieutenant in command of the squad. The short ones were too many for us, and I stood as "I was," thinking of home and the vacant chair, and of Her; so I was wondering if she was thinking of me, and if she would like to be a man, and if she were a man, if she would exchange places with me; and so I was thinking, then the Lieutenant said, "Soldiers! In obedience to the call of our country, our duty, and our Captain, we meet, ready, I see by your countenances, to rush through the imminent breach, or mount the tottering wall. Remember Leonidas and his Spartan few. Remember to preserve—" Silence in ranks!" He abruptly said to stop one of the picked, who was telling the squad how his grandfather had told him how soldiers had been shot crossing the streets in Mexico, which was having a demoralizing effect. "Reinforcements," the Lieutenant continued, "if required, will be sent to us. They are, or are supposed to be holding themselves in readiness at the Military Hall."

One of us asked how many men were there at the arsenal? "Twenty," he replied; "counting the women." I could no longer keep quiet, and falling back on the reserved right of every citizen of the great and glorious country, viz, the right of speech, I asked if our country and our Captain thought it a fair fight, and if our duty compelled us, in our present state of training, to meet the forces of the United States. Why not bring up the reinforcements and make victory certain; why not let me go for the Fourth Brigade? I was willing to volunteer to go on that volunteer hope. Here the fellow who told what his grandfather had told him about shooting soldiers in the streets of Mexico said, his grandfather told him that when he was in the Florida war, they always sent two men or more to carry dispatches, in the case one got killed, and he volunteered to go with me, and so did all of them. As this would have broken up the storming party, the Lieutenant determined not to send for reinforcements. Another fellow proposed that we send to the arsenal to see if they were at home before we called, but the Lieutenant said that was not military; and off to the arsenal gate we marched, and there we halted, pinked, ordered arms, and rested; and there the Lieutenant congratulated us on our steadiness in marching, and the quickness of the march. "For," he said, "we reached here before the gate was shut for the night, otherwise we would have been forced to escalade the fence," which is very dangerous over sharp-pointed fences, and he did not know whether there was a dog inside or not. Then for the first time, we marched in through

Charleston: Day After the Election

Blakely guns and ammunition at the Charleston Arsenal. *Library of Congress.*

the gateway, with heads erect; up to this time the picked had been hanging their heads down, to reduce their height, and dodge shot if necessary, and with no foeman's steel to bar our way, I felt now "Dulce et decorum est pro patria mori." Marching up the pathway, a brother soldier said to me, "You see anything your side?" Looking ahead I saw a field-piece with three men near it. "One on my right saw two," he said, "pointing right at us." Dulce et decorum left me. "Have they arms?" "Two of them have," I replied; "but the third has but one." I have since heard he lost an arm in Mexico.

He whispered to me, "It is an ambush": and while explaining to me— he was an ex-officer of the Beat—what an ambush was, we marched past the guns and the men up into the very centre of the arsenal, and stacked our guns in the barracks of the arsenal, in the building once used as a church...

For the truth of history, I must mention casualties. My breeches, either from the weight of my armament or from my taking too long a breath, broke down behind. I stuck my bayonet through the upper portion of the seat and held them up. What might have been had I not bayonet I would not like to tell. The other was the repulse of a sentinel by a United States cow, which the garrison drove off, crying "Remember Cowpens," and re-established the Post.

And thus on the 7th of November, 1860, was the Charleston Arsenal captured.[6]

CHAPTER 3

Disunion

The South Carolina General Assembly dutifully met on November 9 to discuss secession. Although the debate was intense, the Senate voted 44–1 to let heads cool after the election and agreed to delay a state secession convention until January 15. This was a bitter defeat for the Separate State Secessionists who feared that the momentum created by Lincoln's election would wane if South Carolina waited for other states to declare.

At this point, caution about holding an immediate secession convention might have prevailed had fate not provided the radical conspirators an unexpected windfall. It happened that a banquet celebrating the completion of the Charleston–Savannah railroad had occurred in Savannah on November 3. With a branch office in Savannah, Charleston's shipping magnate Robert Gourdin was among the celebrants. The main speaker was Georgia's prominent Unionist Francis Stebbins Bartow.

Part of Savannah's oligarchy, Bartow was a Whig and a polished orator. He had graduated with highest honors from the University of Georgia in 1835 and went on to study at Yale before returning home to read law with U.S. senator John Berrien. He married Berrien's daughter and became a partner in one of Savannah's finest legal firms. Bartow served two terms in the Georgia House of Representatives and one term in the Georgia Senate. He was a captain in Savannah's elite Oglethorpe Light Infantry.

When Bartow spoke, people listened. At the banquet, he urged South Carolina not to secede because it made no sense for two sovereign states with a long common border to be part of two different nations. He added that

The Mills House, from *Gleason's Pictorial Drawing-Room Companion*. *Courtesy Charleston Museum, Charleston, South Carolina.*

if South Carolina did secede without consulting her neighbor, she had the power of precipitating Georgia into any kind of revolution that she chose. The South Carolinians were charmed by his concession and invited the Georgians to a reciprocal celebration in Charleston on November 9. The ensuing events changed the course of history.

While the legislature was debating in Columbia, Robert Gourdin and the other patrician plotters arranged a princely welcome for Savannah's dignitaries in Charleston. After the Georgians arrived on the new railroad, the city council escorted them aboard the steamer *Carolina* for a luxury tour of Charleston harbor. When the *Carolina* landed, the entourage was driven in the city's finest carriages to the Mills House for a posh two-hundred-person banquet. It was so lavish that the *Charleston Mercury* claimed that it would have satisfied London's Lord Mayor himself. A wide array of sweets followed a feast of turtle soup, turkey, mutton, oysters and turtle steak with wine sauce. Food was washed down with assorted liquors and wines. Mighty shouts filled the air as the crowd grew more boisterous after each speech and toast.

South Carolina Institute Hall and Circular Congregational Church on Meeting Street.
Library of Congress.

By sheer coincidence, November 9 was the same evening that Robert Barnwell Rhett had scheduled a mammoth rally at Institute Hall. After dinner, Gourdin and fellow schemers escorted Francis Bartow and other handpicked Georgians across the street to speak to an assembly of over a thousand men.

Well fed and even more expansive, Bartow spoke again. His oratory electrified the enthusiastic crowd. The reinvented Georgia Unionist now opined that if his neighboring state seceded, South Carolina and Georgia *must* become one nation. His speech was followed by Henry Rootes Jackson,[7] a prominent attorney and prosecutor in Savannah. Another reformed Unionist, Jackson pledged Georgia's support, declaring that they must act without delay. The crowd went wild and demanded an immediate secession convention.

The conspirators lost no time telegraphing the state legislature that Georgia would support South Carolina, and they hired a special train to transport a deputation to Columbia that included the four former federal officials who had recently resigned. Arriving in Columbia at 2:00 p.m. the following day, the delegation from Charleston whipped up support. By 6:00 p.m. that evening, both branches of the legislature had unanimously approved a secession convention date of December 17.

During the tumult, Alfred Aldrich received Senator Hammond's response to his request for an opinion on secession. It was a well-crafted, thirty-five-page anti-disunion epistle. Although the editor of the *Charleston Courier* requested that Aldrich publish the letter, Aldrich suppressed its release, fearing that Hammond's anti-secession letter might jeopardize the legislature's recent reversal. Hammond was contacted and, in spite of disappointment over not having his masterwork published, he went along with the crowd and reluctantly resigned from the U.S. Senate.[8]

> *The atmosphere of Charleston rippled and swelled with excitement all through that memorable fall. The Minute Men, who had organized on every side, made the streets gay with their uniforms, and the young girls devoted their time to manufacturing every kind of patriotic device in palmetto and silk ribbon. Military buttons were in demand, and every young woman was as defiant, as ardent, and as determined, as her brother, or her sweetheart. They were ready for all emergencies, and when the first troops were ordered down to the islands, they packed knapsacks, sewed on straps and buckles, and chattered cheerfully of all things to hide their own dread and sorrow from the older women, the mothers who were sending their all into the great unknown of the future—ready to answer whatever call their country made. The older men met and talked. Constitution, Secession, State Rights, Self-Protection, Union, Usurpation, Imposition.[9]*

Secession fever gripped Charleston. Flags with the state symbol, the palmetto tree, flew on every street and from ships in the harbor. Abraham Lincoln was burned in effigy. News agents vowed never again to sell *Harper's Weekly* because its post-election publication featured a large image of the president-elect.

On December 17, the Secession Convention convened in Columbia in the First Baptist Church. The 169 delegates were the state's power elite: 5 former governors, 40 former state senators, 100 former state representatives and many lawyers. The delegates passed a unanimous resolution to secede from the Union. Due to a smallpox rumor (some suspect it was bogus), the following morning they decided to continue in Charleston and arranged for

Interior of Institute Hall, Charleston, S.C. *Library of Congress.*

an eight-coach train. Arriving at 1:00 p.m. the next day, they were greeted by enthusiastic supporters and a fifteen-gun salute (one for each Southern state).

The convention assembled at 4:00 p.m. at Institute Hall amid a crowd of about seven hundred spectators. After parliamentary procedures, they adjourned at 5:00 p.m. and agreed to meet the following day to draft the ordinance.

On December 19 at 1:00 p.m., the delegates reconvened at St. Andrew's Hall and voted behind closed doors to draft an ordinance for disunion.[10] After the deed was done, someone leaned out the window and gave a sign to the mass of men crowded on Broad Street. When they heard the news, they gave a mighty shout that was said to have swelled until it reached the roar of a tempest, spreading from one end of the city to the other.

The delegates reassembled that evening for a public ceremonial signing. A solemn procession of delegates from St. Andrew's Hall entered Institute Hall accompanied by three thousand cheering onlookers. The Reverend Dr. Bachman gave an invocation beseeching the favor of Almighty God for a blessing on the great act about to be consummated.

The first speaker was Andrew Magrath. He was as dramatic at Institute Hall as he had been in his courtroom, pausing deliberately while his comments

CHARLESTON

MERCURY

EXTRA:

Passed unanimously at 1.15 o'clock, P. M. December 20th, 1860.

AN ORDINANCE

To dissolve the Union between the State of South Carolina and other States united with her under the compact entitled " The Constitution of the United States of America."

We, the People of the State of South Carolina, in Convention assembled, do declare and ordain, and it is hereby declared and ordained,

That the Ordinance adopted by us in Convention, on the twenty-third day of May, in the year of our Lord one thousand seven hundred and eighty-eight, whereby the Constitution of the United States of America was ratified, and also, all Acts and parts of Acts of the General Assembly of this State, ratifying amendments of the said Constitution, are hereby repealed; and that the union now subsisting between South Carolina and other States, under the name of " The United States of America," is hereby dissolved.

THE

UNION

IS

DISSOLVED!

were punctuated by a shout that later became known as the "Rebel Yell." Men tossed their hats into the air and the ring of triumph sounded on every tongue. Cheers grew even louder when Magrath announced that Senator Hammond had just resigned from the Senate.

The animated spectators cheered as each delegate was called forth to solemnly affirm his vote on that fateful document. After the great seal of South Carolina was affixed, the president proclaimed the state of South Carolina a separate, independent nation. The ceremony had lasted two hours. A jubilant crowd greeted the announcement with enthusiasm "beyond the power of the pen" to describe.[11]

Former Senator Hammond was not present that momentous evening. He had resigned primarily out of fear of appearing out of step with his colleagues, especially Senator James Chestnut who had resigned the previous day. As Hammond watched the frenzy in Charleston's streets, he commented that "the scenes of the French Revolution are being enacted already." In his private diary, Hammond confessed that if given a choice between saving the Union and saving slavery, he would choose the Union. He added that the South was wealthy and powerful enough to protect its interests without seceding.

Others shared Hammond's qualms, but with the popular secessionist sentiment, almost none dared to speak openly. The exception was South Carolina's respected Unionist judge James L. Petigru. He is reputed to have said, "South Carolina is too small for a republic, and too large for a lunatic-asylum."

CHAPTER 4

On to Fort Sumter

After secession was declared, the South Carolina General Assembly began enacting the statutes that created a Confederate military. It is estimated that over sixty thousand South Carolina men of military age (18–45) responded to the call to arms and that one-third were killed or lost in action.

The forces of destiny moved quickly. On the night of December 26, on Sullivan's Island, Major Robert Anderson spiked the cannons and set fire to Fort Moultrie.

Covered by darkness, Anderson's garrison of eighty-six men successfully eluded the state's harbor patrol and relocated across the channel to the more defensible Fort Sumter. Still under construction, the fort had only 15 of its 150 guns mounted; the barracks and officer's quarters were unfinished. Surrounded on all sides by South Carolina forces, the isolated troops rushed to complete the installation of additional guns.

Undeterred by Anderson's stealthy withdrawal, patriotic zeal enveloped the citizens of Charleston. On December 27, the Irish Volunteers paraded down the streets and paid their respects to Governor Francis Wilkinson Pickens, who had only recently taken office. Volunteer rifle companies soon occupied Fort Moultrie and the federal fortification at Castle Pinckney.

On December 29, Governor Pickens ordered the Federal Arsenal (under siege since November 7) to be formally occupied by the Scottish Union Light Infantry, under the command of Captain David Ramsay. Shortly thereafter,

Evacuation of Fort Moultrie and burning of the gun carriages on Sullivan's Island, Charleston Harbor, S.C. Artist William Waud, from *Frank Leslie's Illustrated*. *Library of Congress*.

he ordered the Charleston Riflemen, under Captain Joseph Johnson, to the vacant ruins at Fort Johnson on James Island.

With companies from the upcountry flocking to the city, by the middle of January, Charleston had been transformed into a military camp. There was constant drilling and nightly patrols in the streets. Due to the serious nature of the situation, the St. Cecilia and Jockey Club societies gave no balls that year, much to the chagrin of the debutantes who did not have the opportunity to enjoy the season.

Early in January, President Buchanan sent the unarmed *Star of the West* to resupply Fort Sumter. On January 8, under the cover of darkness, *Star of the West* slipped into Charleston Harbor. The following morning, as she headed for Fort Sumter, Citadel cadets on Morris Island fired a warning shot across her bow. When several more shots were fired from Fort Moultrie, the steamer abandoned the mission and returned to her home port of New York Harbor.

In Washington, Mrs. Anderson was so concerned for her husband's welfare that she found Peter Hart, Anderson's old sergeant, and had him escort her to Charleston. She was able to persuade Governor Pickens to

Interior view of Castle Pinckney, directly across from the Battery in Charleston Harbor. *Library of Congress.*

let her visit her husband at the fort. Her trip was so stressful that when she returned to Washington, she promptly collapsed from the exertions.

Exactly one month after the firing on *Star of the West*, the Confederate States of America was formed.

Charlestonians were on edge. In the days that led up to the shelling of Fort Sumter, more than three thousand men from across South Carolina assembled in the city. In March, the newly formed Confederate government sent Brigadier General P.G.T. Beauregard to take command of Charleston's defenses; he immediately directed strengthening the batteries around the harbor.

Firing on the *Star of the West*. *Harper's Weekly*.

Abraham Lincoln was inaugurated March 4, 1861. In his inaugural speech, he promised not to interfere with slavery, but added that he would not tolerate secession. Most Charlestonians were outraged at Lincoln's address and considered his remarks practically a declaration of war. Their mood was ugly.

Lincoln determined to take whatever actions were necessary to preserve government property in the states that had recently seceded. He thought that Fort Sumter could hold out until things were resolved, but the day after his inauguration, he received a letter from Anderson advising just how critical the situation was.

On March 13, retired naval officer and trusted friend Captain Gustavus V. Fox gave Lincoln a plan to re-provision and reinforce Fort Sumter. Fox visited Anderson on March 21 and told him of the possibility of a relief expedition. He returned to Washington with the intelligence that the fort could hold out only until April 15.

Lincoln also sent Ward Hill Lamon and Stephen A. Hurlbut to Charleston to assess the situation. Lamon was Lincoln's former law partner and self-appointed personal bodyguard. (Lamon had accompanied Lincoln on the midnight train through Baltimore after Allan Pinkerton discovered a secessionist plot to kill Lincoln before the inauguration.) Lamon was a big burly man who had just been appointed a federal marshal in the District of Columbia. His arrival was noted by the local citizenry. He clandestinely visited James L. Petigru and conferred with Governor Pickens, who told him in no uncertain terms that reinforcing the beleaguered fort meant war. Lamon intimated to the governor that Fort Sumter would be abandoned, a notion that was shared by many in both the North and South.

Stephen A. Hurlbut, a native Charlestonian who had disgraced himself financially before he fled to Illinois, was a poor choice for an emissary.[12] When Lamon returned to the Mills House after visiting Anderson at Fort Sumter, locals almost lynched the pair before they were hastily escorted to the railroad station. Back in Washington, both men informed Lincoln that attempting to relieve Fort Sumter would result in war.

Lincoln met with his cabinet on March 29 and issued a secret order to prepare for a naval expedition to Charleston. He instructed Captain Fox to make plans to relieve the fort.

On April 8, a government envoy personally read Lincoln's message to Governor Pickens: "I am directed by the President of the United States to notify you to expect an attempt will be made to supply Fort Sumter with provisions only, and that if such an attempt be not resisted, no effort to throw in men, arms, or ammunition will be made without further notice, or in case of an attack upon the Fort."

Governor Pickens forwarded the message to Jefferson Davis, who immediately went into an emergency session with his cabinet. Only the secretary of state, Robert Toombs,[13] voiced reservations, stating prophetically: "The firing on that fort will inaugurate a civil war greater than any the world has yet seen…at this time it is suicide, murder, and you will lose us every friend in the North. You will wantonly strike a hornet's nest that extends from the mountains to the ocean. Legions now quiet will swarm our state and sting us to death. It is unnecessary. It puts us in the wrong. It is fatal."

Davis did not agree and ordered General Beauregard to demand Fort Sumter's evacuation and, if refused, to reduce it. Beauregard immediately asked for a delay, but Davis was emphatic, permitting the general only the opportunity to give Anderson a definite time for surrender.

As the relief ships headed south, the ill-kept secret was published across the land. In Charleston, General Beauregard intercepted correspondence that confirmed that Anderson knew relief was on the way. The following day the Confederate government decided to take action before the fleet arrived and ordered Beauregard to proceed.

On April 11, Beauregard learned that the ships were not far from Charleston and sent his aide-de-camp Colonel James Chestnut, the former U.S. senator, and Captain Stephen D. Lee to Fort Sumter to demand surrender. Anderson refused and asked to be notified when the firing would commence.

Beauregard had once been Anderson's pupil at West Point and tried to extend him every courtesy. Still hoping to avoid bloodshed, Beauregard's aides returned to Fort Sumter after midnight to inquire when Anderson would be starved out and could surrender honorably. Stalling for time, the major finally replied that they would be forced to evacuate by April 15.

Unable to delay any longer, Colonel Chestnut wrote Anderson a note at 3:20 a.m. notifying him that the Confederate batteries would open fire in an hour's time.

It is uncertain who gave the order to commence firing. On April 12 at 4:30 a.m., the batteries in the forts surrounding the harbor began the bombardment.

Only the guns in Charleston were silent, permitting the whole community to crowd the Battery and adjacent houses to witness the spectacle.

> *With strained eyes, or the aid of opera glasses, telescopes—whatever one was fortunate enough to possess—for two days* [they] *watched the bloodless battle, wondering what would be the fate of* [their] *loved ones, for every house sent its youth; there was scarcely a family that had not at least one son in the fight. Slowly and steadily our batteries fired, and sullenly Sumter answered them; and when, on the second day, the white flag was hoisted, on all sides came the cry, "They surrender! They surrender!" This first battle of the war had many trying circumstances connected with it—those on whom our guns were turned had lived among us as friends and honored guests, and all in one day, as it were, they became deadly enemies.* [14]

The Union warships made no attempt to relieve the fort during the attack. Outmanned and outgunned, Anderson surrendered his command on the thirteenth and evacuated Fort Sumter the following day. Miraculously, no one was killed. Soldiers at the Confederate forts cheered Sumter's brave defenders. While the city celebrated its great victory, the curious obtained boats to see the vanquished fort firsthand.

After the fall of Sumter, nearly all the volunteer companies were relieved from duty, and a season of recreation followed.

The floating battery was constructed of pine heartwood buttressed by palmetto logs on the bow. Located off Sullivan's Island, it was used in the bombardment of Fort Sumter. *Frank Leslie's Illustrated.*

"The Battery or Park Promenade at Charleston, South Carolina, during the bombardment of Fort Sumter." (*Harper's Weekly*, May 18, 1861.) *Courtesy Charleston Museum, Charleston, South Carolina.*

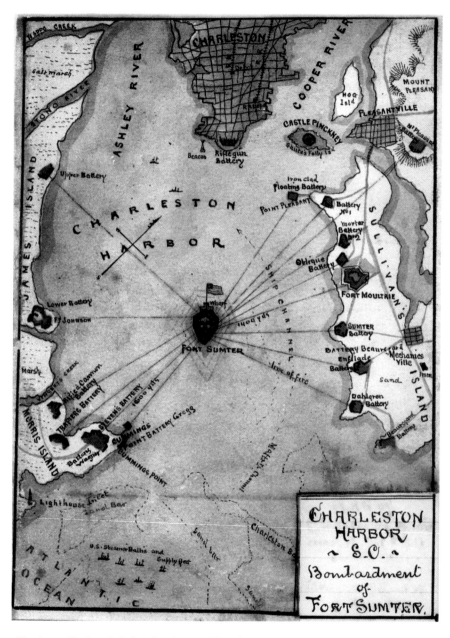

Charleston Harbor, S.C. Bombardment of Fort Sumter. (Note floating Battery just off Sullivan's Island.) *Library of Congress.*

An elegant fête champetre, in honor of General Beauregard, was given by Mr. Wm. Izard Bull, at his beautiful home, Ashley Hall, which had been the home of the Bulls since colonial days, when Governor Bull was one of the Governors of the Province of Carolina. Ashley Hall, on this April day, seemed to have donned its fairest dress, as though there could not be too much beauty to do honor to the occasion; or perhaps there was foreknowledge that this would be the last fête day under those grand old oaks! though no such feeling clouded the gayety of those who joined the brilliant throng that day, and in spite of there being comparatively few civilians to be seen, none seemed to realize that grim-visaged war was near at hand, and that ere the close of the year, many of those with us would have sacrificed their lives on the altar of their country![15]

CHAPTER 5

The Anaconda Plan

When the shots were fired in Charleston, Mexican War hero lieutenant general Winfield Scott was the nation's highest ranking officer. He was seventy-four years old and plagued with severe health problems. He also weighed over three hundred pounds, a handicap that made it impossible for him to mount a horse or lead troops into battle.

Scott considered Colonel Robert E. Lee of Virginia the finest officer in the nation. A graduate of West Point, Lee had served in the Corps of Engineers for seventeen years. He did not believe in secession and hoped his home state would stay in the Union. Scott offered him command of the Federal army on April 17. This was the same day that Virginia voted to leave the Union. Rather than fight his fellow Virginians, Lee resigned his commission and accepted the command of Virginia's troops. Command of the Federal field forces passed to Brigadier General Irvin McDowell.

On April 19, five days after the bombardment of Fort Sumter, President Abraham Lincoln issued a proclamation that declared all ports of the seceded states (South Carolina, Georgia, Alabama, Florida, Mississippi, Louisiana and Texas) would be blockaded. "If…a vessel shall approach, or shall attempt to leave…said ports, she will be duly warned by the Commander of one of the blockading vessels, who will endorse on her register the fact and date of such warning, and if the same vessel shall again attempt to enter or leave the blockaded port, she will be captured and sent to the nearest convenient port, for such proceedings against her and her cargo as prize, as may be deemed advisable." (North Carolina and Virginia were added once they seceded.)

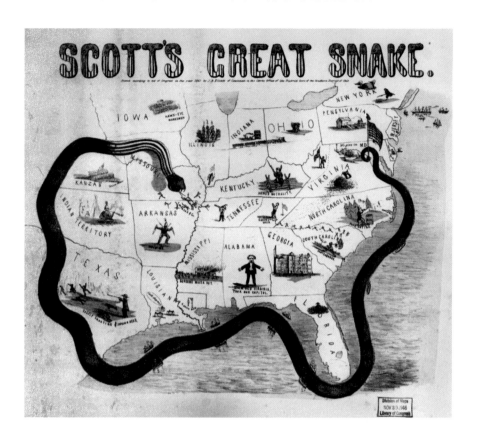

After the humiliating defeat at Manassas in July, Northern politicians and the press clamored for a quick victory. Lincoln conferred with Scott about a war strategy. Scott felt that the best way to subdue the agrarian South was to squeeze off its European supply lines and its export capabilities. He proposed a plan to utilize the blockade system and simultaneously outflank the Confederate armies by taking the Mississippi River and Tennessee River Valley. Dubbed the Anaconda Plan, this slow war of attrition was scorned by those who demanded a quick victory; however, Scott's plan was ultimately adopted.

Sealing off 3,500 miles of Confederate coastline was no small task. Charged with overseeing the effort was Secretary of the Navy Gideon Welles,[16] who lost no time in putting the blockade in motion. Welles recalled all warships from abroad, purchased civilian and merchant ships and retrofitted them for war and ordered a massive shipbuilding program.

In addition, Salmon P. Chase, secretary of the treasury, persuaded Welles to set up a commission to study the Confederate coastline. The

Blockade Strategy Board was established in late June 1861. Members were distinguished in their respective fields. Captain Samuel Francis DuPont had become a midshipman before the Naval Academy had been established; he had enjoyed a long career in the navy before he became the Blockade Strategy Board chairman. Endeavoring to make global waterways more navigable, Commander Charles Henry Davis had spent his career studying tidal action. Major John Gross Barnard, a West Point graduate in the Army Corps of Engineers was chief engineer of the District of Washington. Alexander Dallas Bache, another West Point graduate, was in the U.S. Coast Survey where he had overseen coastal fortifications and conducted a detailed survey mapping of the United States coastline.

The Blockade Strategy Board issued their first report on Fernandia, Florida, on July 5. By July 13, they had completed their report on the South Carolina coast, and by mid-September, they had completed their study of the Mississippi River and Gulf Coast.

To enforce the blockade, Union naval ships were assigned areas of operation. In October 1861, the Atlantic Operation was split into the North Atlantic Blockading Squadron, based at Hampton Roads, Virginia, covering Virginia and North Carolina, and the South Atlantic Blockading Squadron, covering the area from Cape Henry, Virginia, to Key West, Florida. The Gulf Blockading Squadron patrolled the coast from Key West to the Mexican border; it was split into two squadrons in early 1862. The West Gulf Blockading Squadron was created when the Gulf Blockading Squadron was split.

The Lincoln administration accepted the board's recommendations for the Atlantic blockade with only one major modification. The natural advantages of Port Royal Sound were so great that the administration diverged from the board's original plan. Lack of knowledge of the Gulf coast caused greater divergence in the west. Ship Island was taken according to plan and became the staging ground for the assault and capture of New Orleans in April 1862.

The blockade succeeded in closing all major Confederate ports. Port Royal fell in November 1861; Fernandina, Florida, was taken the following month. In April 1862, Savannah was sealed by the surrender of Fort Pulaski, and New Orleans surrendered that same month. Charleston was shut down in 1863, and Mobile Bay was captured in August 1864. Wilmington, North Carolina, the last open Confederate port, was closed down when its coastal defense system collapsed with the fall of Fort Fisher in January 1865. The Confederate States of America collapsed shortly thereafter.

CHAPTER 6

Sinking of the
Great Stone Fleet

Charleston was the South's second-largest city. With good railroad and steamboat connections, it quickly became one of the chief ports of entry for Confederate war materiel.

Northerners had come to hate "the cradle of secession," and called Charleston a "rat hole." The blockade started in May 1861, but Union warships patrolling beyond the reach of Charleston's forts had not been able to impede commerce due to the harbor's numerous navigable channels. Popular Northern sentiment was to bring arrogant Charleston to its knees!

Re-enter Gustavis Fox, recently elevated to the position of assistant secretary of the navy and still smarting that his ships had arrived too late to relieve Fort Sumter before the bombardment. Fox was determined to shut down Charleston. His unorthodox solution was to destroy the harbor by scuttling a fleet of old boats in the shipping channels.

Secretary of the Navy Gideon Welles liked the idea and secretly began purchasing a fleet of New England whalers. (Due to the recent discovery of petroleum, the whaling industry was in decline.) Later known as "the rat-hole squadron" or "the stone fleet," the old whalers averaged three hundred tons. The Union paid about $10 per ton, considered a good price for junk ships. Some of the better vessels fetched as much as $4,000.

The Navy also purchased 7,500 tons of granite at fifty cents a ton. In addition to the blocks of quarried rock, the tempting prices had attracted fieldstones collected from old pasture walls and abandoned foundations dotting the rocky farms near the New England coast.

The officer selected to head the expedition was recently promoted Captain Charles Henry Davis,[17] DuPont's chief of staff during the stunning capture of Port Royal. Before the war, Captain Davis had served on the Charleston harbor improvement commission. He was familiar with the tides and currents and knew exactly where to sink the whalers. Not wanting to destroy a good harbor, Davis wrote his wife, "This is a disagreeable duty, and one of the last I should have selected." He called the venture "the maggot [that] got into Fox's brain."[18]

Amazingly, the mission was kept secret until the day the fleet set sail. On November 21, amid a cheering crowd, thirteen ships sailed out of New London, Connecticut; another twelve were cheered as they left New Bedford and Boston.

Papers picked up the story immediately. On November 23, the *New York Times* published "THE STONE BLOCKADE; Sailing of the Fleet of Old Whalers to be Sunk Across the Southern Harbors Copy of the Secret Orders List of Vessels, &c." The article was amazingly detailed and also reprinted the secret orders to each ship's captain.

They are all old, but substantial, whaling vessels, double-decked, to give them greater firmnees. They were stripped of their copper and other fittings, which were not necessary for so short a voyage as they will make, and loaded with picked stone, as deeply as was safe. They were purchased by the Government at New-Bedford, New-London, Nantucket, Sag Harbor, Edgartown, Mystic and Newport. In the bottom of each ship a hole was bored, into which was fitted a lead pipe five inches in diameter, with a valve so fixed that, though perfectly safe even for a long voyage, it can be very quickly removed. It is calculated that the ship will be filled and sunk to the bottom in twenty minutes after the removal of this valve. To provide against accidental jamming of the valves, each vessel is furnished with two augurs of the proper size.

The crews consist of six men each. These will be returned by the men of war, who will assist in the work of sinking. Each ship will be anchored in the place chosen for her, and will then be sprung round broadside to the channel, thus effecting as great a stoppage as is possible. When this is done, and she is in position, the valve will be withdrawn, and when the vessel is nearly level with the water's edge, the men will leave in a small boat. The captains of the ships are all well acquainted with our coast, first-rate seamen and good pilots.

The December 14 *Harper's Weekly* published an oversized illustration of the Stone Fleet en route with an accompanying article entitled "The Rat-Hole Squadron."

The original plan had been to send some of the fleet to blockade Savannah and then proceed to Charleston. When the Confederates sank three steamers in the Savannah River to stop their progress, the aging vessels joined the ships waiting at Port Royal and continued on to Charleston. Under the direction of Admiral DuPont, on December 18, the convoy approached the bar opposite Morris Island. To thwart their plans, the Confederates blew up the lighthouses and tore down harbor beacons.

According to the *New York Times*, the weather was delightful the day of the sinking, and a soft breeze tempered the heat of the sun. "Adding to the picturesqueness of the scene were the tents and store-houses on the distant shore, and the fleet of transports and naval vessels at anchor in the inner roadstead...the sunset, too, was splendid." The *Times* correspondent moralized:

> *The main channel of approach to Charleston harbor has been destroyed. Sixteen stone-filled hulks, placed checker wise across the passage, in the deepest water, just at the inner and outer edges of the bar, are the mediums through which this righteous retribution has been measured out. Thus another strong blow has fallen upon the headstrong people of South Carolina, the effect of which must be more humiliating than any they have yet received. They have no means of resenting it, and their haughty rebellious spirits must fret and chafe beneath the weight of the heavy hand which has been laid upon them.*[19]

The January 11, 1862 *Harper's Weekly* waxed eloquent:

> *At half past four this afternoon (December 19), the tide being nearly full, we recrossed the bar and ran a hawser to the bark Theodosia, of New London, which was to be the first victim, and towed her across the bar to the upper boat, on the left-hand side of the channel. When we had her in a good position, Captain Stevens, through a speaking-trumpet, ordered the captain to "cast off the hawser."*
>
> *"Ay, ay, Sir." came back the reply and the hawser was let go and roused in again on our deck in the twinkling of an eye. The trembling old bark, being under some headway, moved slowly on to the exact spot we wished her, and then struck the bottom; and her anchor dropped for the last time in the water,*

"Sinking the Stone Fleet in Charleston Harbor." (*Harper's Weekly*, January 11, 1862.)

the chain rattling out as cheerfully as any chain might which had made its last run, and the old bark settled down into its own grave. The plug had been knocked out as the anchor dropped, and the water rushed madly and wildly in. In a moment the whale-boats were lowered and alongside, and the dunnage of the officers and crew rapidly passed over the bulwarks and into them.

We did not wait for them, but hurried out, to tow in another before dark. The first ship touched bottom and the plug was drawn as the sun went down.

The Rebecca Simms was towed in and anchored at the other side of the channel, and the water soon filled her hold, and she sank slowly and in a dignified manner, rocking uneasily, to be sure, as the water poured in, but going down with every rope and spar in place, as a brave man falls in battle, with his harness on.

We had now got the position of the bar clearly marked out, and the Florida's boats were relieved from their unpleasant position as buoys, and they returned to their ship. Our work was reported to Captain Davis, and he requested the Pocahontas and the Ottawa to tow in and sink all the ships they could after the moon had risen high enough to afford us light to see.

At eight o'clock we were again at work. We towed in and sunk four more before the low water made it impossible for the loaded ships to be placed in position, and then we ran out again and anchored outside the bar.

The Pocahontas towed in two during the evening. While we were at work, the harbor was dotted with whale-boats, running from their respective ships to the Cahawba, carrying away their (the officers' and crews') baggage and the valuable sails and furniture of the ships. Some of the men-of-war boats were engaged in visiting the sunken ships and securing flour, potatoes, onions, and other acceptable provisions, rope, furniture, etc…

On the following day he writes again:

I have frequently read of masts going by the board on ships at sea in a gale of wind, but never saw the deed performed till today. It is certainly worth witnessing, where you have not the accompaniments of a howling gale, a wild mountain sea, and a groaning ship, leaking at every joint beneath you. Under those circumstances the cutting away masts may afford a sense of relief, but none of gratification or pleasure…but what is now the seat of rebellion, and an object of just revenge, the dismasting of the hulks, within sight of the rebel flags and rebel guns, is really an unalloyed pleasure. One feels that at least one cursed rat-hole has been closed, and one avenue of supplies cut off by the hulks, and anything that adds to the efficiency of the work affords additional pleasure. Most of the ships in sinking had listed to one side, and the masts, of course, stood at an angle over their sides.

The braces and shrouds on the weather side were cut by the sharp axe of the whaleman, and the tall masts, swaying for an instant, fell together with a loud crash, the sticks snapping like brittle pipe-stems close to the deck, and striking the water like an avalanche, beating it into a foam and throwing the spray high into the air. For an hour or two this crashing, smashing sound was heard on every side, and one after another ship became a mere hulk upon the waters. All were dismasted save the Robin Hood, which was spared for another purpose.

The scene presented in the harbor when the work was done was novel and interesting. Here were fifteen dismasted hulks, in every possible position, lying across the channel—some on their port, others on their starboard sides. Some were under water forward, others aft. The sea swept over some of them ; others stood on upright keels, and spouted water from their sides, as the heavy swells raised them and dropped them heavily down upon the sand again; and proudly, among them all, was the East Indiaman, brave Robin Hood, with her graceful, tapering masts towering aloft, and apparently still afloat.

The *Robin Hood* was set ablaze after the deed was done, much to the delight of the seamen aboard the blockaders.

The mission became controversial almost immediately. Northern newspapers may have applauded the stone fleet as an acceptable act of war, but the sinking stirred up European maritime powers more than any event of the war other than the *Trent* Affair. Robert E. Lee, who was in Charleston at the time, wrote Secretary of War Judah P. Benjamin, "This achievement, so unworthy of any nation, is the abortive expression of the malice and revenge of a people."

Although the wreckage temporarily blocked the main channel, blockade runners were still able to slip through Maffitt's Channel near Sullivan's Island. To block that passage, a second fleet of barks and brigs was sunk January 25–26, 1863, off Rattlesnake Shoals near present-day Isle of Palms.[20]

Captain Davis's assessment that the obstructions would have no lasting impact proved correct. In spite of the mass of hulks, skillful blockade runners were still able to enter and exit Charleston harbor. Within four months, spring tides had washed the stones out to sea. Ironically, the stones were said to have deepened the shipping lanes. Herman Melville's poem "The Stone Fleet—An Old Sailor's Last Lament" said it all, "A failure, and complete, Was your Old Stone Fleet."[21]

CHAPTER 7

The Company that Went to War

By 1860, John Fraser and Company was one of Charleston's leading cotton exporters and enjoyed a far-flung international trade. The firm was located at the North Central Wharf at the foot of Cumberland Street; it boasted immense warehouses and long rows of offices. In its heyday, the company could handle twenty thousand bales of cotton in a morning. In 1854, they commissioned two 767-ton ships specifically designed for the Charleston–Liverpool trade, and in 1860, they proudly advertised an exclusive line of monthly Charleston–Liverpool sailing packets.

John Fraser died in 1854, leaving George Alfred Trenholm (1807–1876) in charge of the firm. Trenholm had worked his way up from rather unpromising prospects. His grandfather, William Trenholm, had been a Loyalist who had immigrated to Holland during the Revolutionary War. The family returned to Charleston in 1787 after a brief sojourn in Santo Domingo. According to family tradition, William's son was a sea captain who returned to Santo Domingo to marry the daughter of the Comte de Greffin, a French landowner. Upon discovering that she had already married, he wed her sister Irene. The couple had seven children.

Upon his father's death, George Trenholm's formal education stopped. He became an accountant and at age seventeen found himself supporting five younger siblings. He began working for John Fraser and Company in 1835, and by the time Trenholm became senior partner, it was a consortium with interlocking directorates with Trenholm Brothers in New York City and Fraser, Trenholm & Company in Liverpool. The firm's copartners were

John Fraser, Edward L. Trenholm, Theodore Wagner, James T. Welsman and Charles Kuhn Prioleau.

George Trenholm had major interests in banking circles and was part owner and president of the Bank of Charleston. In 1830, he began to write under the pseudonym "Mercator," penning numerous articles supporting the construction of a railroad between Louisville, Cincinnati and Charleston. He served on the board of the Blue Ridge Railroad before and after the war.[22]

Trenholm became involved in politics and espoused the states' rights policies of John C. Calhoun; he was elected to the South Carolina House of Representatives in 1852 but later resigned because of an unintended conflict of interest. He represented Charleston three other times in the 1850s and 1860s. After the war started, he was elected one of the commissioners for the defense of the state and was on the committee to build the ironclad steamboats financed by Charleston merchants. He replaced C.G. Memminger as secretary of the treasury shortly before the fall of the Confederacy.[23] In his prime, he was described as the "absolute master of local banking and the cotton trade."[24]

Once hostilities started, Trenholm Brothers in New York City was closed, and branch offices under other names were set up in Nassau and Bermuda. Ownership of many Trenholm vessels was transferred to British registry. At one point, Trenholm firms either owned outright or had interest in 120 merchant ships.

INTRIGUE IN LIVERPOOL

Because the South lacked the infrastructure to manufacture more than a few warships, Secretary of the Navy Stephen Mallory sent James Dunwoody Bulloch to Liverpool to oversee naval acquisitions in the British Empire. Bulloch was from a distinguished Georgia family and had served in the United States Navy for fifteen years before joining a private shipping company in 1854. He was in New Orleans when Fort Sumter fell and immediately offered his services to the Confederacy. Secretary Mallory jumped at the chance of having a foreign agent with a naval background and familiarity with international trade. Although Bulloch would have preferred to command a ship, he accepted the post of naval procurement agent and headed for Liverpool.

Section from a panorama of Liverpool drawn from a balloon in 1865. In the center are Wellington Monument and the elegant St. George's Hall, where Mary Elizabeth Prioleau organized several balls to raise money for Confederate wounded.

In 1861, Liverpool was the world's largest port and was considered the "second city of the British Empire." Some 60 percent of the South's cotton went through Liverpool to the Lancashire cotton mills. The city's vast waterfront was lined with shipyards and docks; the urban area was adorned with numerous handsome buildings. The city prided itself on its sophistication and elegant mansions. Although Britain was officially neutral and laws forbade supplying any means of war, there was a lot of support for the Southern cause and the burgeoning wartime commerce.

Bulloch sailed into Liverpool on June 3 and immediately commenced what is considered the greatest clandestine operation of the nineteenth century. With a $1 million budget, his initial assignment was the purchase of six steam propeller vessels through the offices of Fraser, Trenholm & Company.

The first contract was a cruiser built at the shipyard of William C. Miller & Sons in Toxteth. Although alleged to be owned by an Italian firm, hull #345 did not go unnoticed by Union spies who regularly reported to Thomas

The inauspicious façade of Fraser, Trenholm & Company at 10 Rumfort Place belied the cloak-and-dagger activities conducted behind its closed doors. *Courtesy Ethel Nepveux.*

Dudley, the U.S. consul. Dudley, in turn, reported his concerns to Charles Francis Adams, the minister to Britain and son and grandson of two U.S. presidents. Dudley feared that when fully armed, the emerging vessel could be a formidable foe. Seriously alarmed, Ambassador Adams complained to the British Foreign Office. To placate him, the vessel, by then named *Oreto*, was inspected by customs officials who found everything in proper order.

Manned by an English master and crew, on March 22, 1862, *Oreto* sailed out of Liverpool for a festive excursion complete with ladies aboard to make Union agents think that she was on a trial run. After putting the ladies ashore, *Oreto* headed for Nassau, where she was handed over to John Newland Maffit. Once commissioned as the CSS *Florida*, she proceeded to destroy forty-six vessels before she was captured illegally in neutral Bahia, Brazil, in October 1864.

In July 1861, a second ship (hull #290, later CSS *Alabama*) was commissioned through Fraser, Trenholm & Company, this time at Laird's shipyard in Birkenhead. Charles Prioleau, head of the Liverpool office, personally managed the clandestine operation. He bought the furnishings, financed the ships that took the armaments out to sea and paid all expenses the entire time the cruiser was in service. The specialty ship was designed to be capable of sustaining itself independent of foreign ports, with extra space for 350 tons of coal, stores, provisions, repair parts and tools. The ship could make up to 10 knots under sail alone and 13.25 knots when sail and steam power were used together.

To keep tabs on #290, Dudley hired a private detective and a team of spies to obtain information from Laird's workers. In spite of his complaints, everything appeared in order and British officials permitted #290 to have her engines and boilers installed and launched as *Enrica*.

On July 29, 1862, Bulloch learned that *Enrica* was about to be seized. Once again he hastily assembled a group for a festive sea trial. With guests on board, *Enrica* slipped down the Mersey River accompanied by the tug *Hercules*. Late in the afternoon, Bulloch informed the visitors that *Enrica* needed to be out all night for trials and accompanied his charges back to port on the *Hercules*. (British authorities issued a hold order on *Enrica* two days after she left port. The escape became an embarrassment to the British government, which later prohibited the launching of two ironclad rams Bulloch then had under construction at Lairds.)

Meanwhile, *Enrica* sailed to the Azores. Shortly thereafter, the Confederate captain, Raphael Semmes, some of the Confederate officers and Bulloch left aboard the steamer *Bahama*, arriving at Terceira Island on August 20, 1862.

Semmes had been given command of the new cruiser after his previous command was put out of commission. *Sumter* had sunk or captured eighteen ships before she was finally bottled up in the Spanish port of Algesiras. Instead of trying to escape, Semmes abandoned the trapped ship, and three months later, he and his crew were safely back in England ready for more action. (In December 1862, *Sumter* was disarmed and sold at auction to Fraser-Trenholm interests and continued service under British colors as the blockade runner *Gibraltar*.)

Before leaving Liverpool, Bulloch had arranged to rendezvous with the supply vessel *Agrippina*, which had in her hold provisions, armaments and more coal. It took three days of backbreaking work by all three crews to transform *Enrica* into a Confederate warship. Commissioned on August 24, 1862, CSS *Alabama* immediately started wreaking havoc on the U.S. whaling fleet, destroying ten ships within the next two weeks.[25]

(Stephen Mallory had promised Bulloch command of the new cruiser after *Oreto*—later *Florida*—left England. Thinking the ship would soon be his,

Captain Semmes and Lieutenant Kell aboard CSS *Alabama* in Cape Town. According to Evan P. Jones, captain of the *Deerhound*, Kell was Semmes's mainstay and chief counselor, and he owed much of his success and reputation to Kell's sagacity and promptness of resource. The 1864 Cape Town visit passed into South African folklore in the Afrikaans song, "*Daar Kom die Alibama.*" *U.S. Navy Photo.*

Bulloch had painstakingly overseen the construction details of hull #290. Unfortunately for Bulloch, Secretary Mallory reneged on his promise because he felt that nobody else could fill his shoes. It was small consolation that his half brother, Irvine Stephens Bulloch, served as *Alabama*'s Sailing Master.)[26]

During her time at sea, *Alabama*'s crew boarded 386 vessels and burned 66 Union vessels, mostly merchant ships, valued at $6,547,000. *Alabama* captured two thousand prisoners without a single loss of life; captured ships' crews and passengers were detained only until they could be placed aboard a neutral ship or put ashore in a friendly port. Spanning the globe, *Alabama* never visited a Confederate port. By June 1864, *Alabama* had been at sea for 534 days and headed into Cherbourg, France, for badly needed maintenance.

BATTLE OF THE CENTURY

U.S. Navy secretary Gideon Wells had assigned twenty-five ships to search for *Alabama*, at a staggering cost of $7 million. John Ancrum Winslow, captain of the

Captain John A. Winslow, USN. *Library of Congress.*

screw-sloop-of-war USS *Kearsarge*, was off the coast of Holland when he learned of *Alabama*'s whereabouts through the U.S. minister to France. Eager for battle, *Kearsarge* hastened to Cherbourg. (To protect her boilers, *Kearsarge* had installed anchor chain cable triced in tiers over her port and starboard midsections.)

Winslow sailed into Cherbourg, and once he was assured that the *Alabama* was safely contained, he waited offshore for his adversary. Captain Semmes's practice had been "hit and run" instead of direct confrontation, but with his ship trapped, he chose to fight and sent a bold challenge to Winslow through diplomatic channels. "My intention is to fight the *Kearsarge* as soon as I can make the necessary arrangements. I hope these will not detain me more than until to-morrow or the morrow morning at farthest. I beg she will not depart until I am ready to go out. I have the honor to be Your obedient servant, R. Semmes, Captain."

For the next few days, Semmes and Winslow diligently drilled their crews and put their affairs in order. Semmes took the added precaution of taking ashore four sacks containing the accumulation of *Alabama*'s long cruise: 4,700 gold sovereigns, 6 million francs in currency and $20,000 in ingots, comprising the ransom bonds of ten ships he had released because he had no room aboard *Alabama* for their crews, plus a valuable collection of captured ships' chronometers.

Before the battle, the *Gazette des Etrangers* wrote:

> *There was something fatal in the aspect of this audacious vessel. She was coming from the Cape of Good Hope, implacable enemy of all Federal vessels, loaded with gold, bruised, disabled, exhausted, having sown death on her way and slaughtered all. Even the uniformly grey uniforms of the crew seemed grave and significant in effect...death seemed to hover already over this vessel, which the finger of God had designated...While others were dancing on the beach these brave men were getting ready to die.*[27]

On Sunday morning, June 19, *Alabama* steamed out of Cherbourg escorted by the French ironclad *Couronne*, which stayed in the area to ensure that the combat remained in international waters. In her wake trailed the English *Deerhound*, a small steamer flying the flag of the Royal Mersey Yacht Club.

> *As the Alabama approached, Kearsarge steamed further to sea, to ensure that Alabama could not easily return to port...At 10:50 AM, Captain Winslow put his ship around and headed for the enemy. Alabama opened fire a few minutes later, at a distance of about a mile, and continued to fire as the range decreased. As the ships closed to about a half-mile, Kearsarge turned and began to shoot back...Both ships had their guns trained to starboard, and the engagement followed a circular course, with the ships steaming in opposite directions and turning to counter the other's attempts to gain an advantageous position.*[28]

Kearsarge was burning Newcastle coals and *Alabama* Welsh coals, which burned differently and made it easy to track the movements of each ship.

The protective chain armor and superior gunnery of the *Kersarge* soon began to tell. Although *Alabama* hit her opponent several times, the deteriorated condition of her powder and shells caused little damage. Sensing that the battle was lost, Semmes attempted to sail to the French coast, but a shell entered the ship at the water line and exploded in the boiler room. With his ship taking in water, Semmes ordered the flag lowered to escape further fire from the enemy. Some junior officers, including Irvine Bulloch, began firing the port guns after *Alabama* struck her colors. After another broadside from *Kearsarge*, a white flag appeared over the stern, whereupon Captain Winslow ordered a cease-fire. The entire battle lasted one hour and two minutes.

During the engagement, Semmes's right arm was wounded by a shell fragment. With *Alabama* sinking rapidly, he ordered the wounded crewmen and those who did not know how to swim put into lifeboats, put on a life jacket and joined the rest of the crew who had stripped down before plunging into the water. Two loyal crewmen volunteered to retrieve *Alabama*'s papers and swam one-armed to nearby rescue vessels, all the while holding the ship's documents above their heads.

"The *Alabama*'s final plunge was a remarkable freak…She shot up out of the water bow first, and descended on the same line, carrying away with her plunge two of her masts, and making a whirlpool of considerable size and strength"[29] that sucked down several nearby men. Fortunately, they were able to resurface.

With some of his lifeboats damaged during the battle, Winslow used a bullhorn to ask the nearby *Deerhound* to help rescue survivors. *Kearsarge*'s launch searched for the celebrated Semmes and asked *Deerhound*'s lifeboat if Semmes had been rescued. Mr. Kell, *Alabama*'s first officer, had disguised himself by putting on a hat with *Deerhound* emblazoned on it and had taken up an oar. He informed the search party that Semmes had drowned. (Referred to by his crew as "Old Beeswax," Semmes was easily identifiable by his waxed handlebar mustache, and it was Kell who had recommended that Semmes lie flat in the bottom of the boat.)

Deerhound rescued forty-two of *Alabama*'s officers and crew. Instead of turning the survivors over as prisoners of war, *Deerhound* boldly kept the English flag flying and turned toward home. *Deerhound* extended every kindness to the survivors, even supplying dry clothing to the exhausted and half-clad men.[30] Much to the distress of his crew, Captain Winslow was

"The Sinking of the Pirate *Alabama.*" From nineteenth-century sheet music. *Library of Congress.*

forced to watch his would-be prisoners escape, for he refused to fire on the neutral vessel.

En route to Southampton, *Deerhound* passed the sailing yacht *Hornet* carrying other survivors; one remarked that they had aboard all their treasure, including the sixty chronometers.

When accused of purposely following the battle so that he could rescue Semmes and his crew, John Lancaster, the owner of the *Deerhound* explained, "The fact is, that when we passed the *Kearsarge*, the captain cried out, 'For God's sake, do what you can to save them,' and that was my warrant for interfering in any way for the aid and succor of his enemies." (*Deerhound* was sold later to Sir George Stuckley and in 1869 became the first British yacht to enter the Suez Canal. Sold again, she helped rescue many slaves in Zanzibar before going down in a storm.)

The naval duel was one of the most widely watched sea battles in history. A special excursion train from Paris brought hundreds of pleasure-seekers to witness the spectacle. In addition, a new casino had opened in Cherbourg that weekend, and the hotels were overflowing. In a circus-like atmosphere, peddlers hawked outrageously priced binoculars, camp stools and Confederate flags. Betting was brisk, with *Alabama* heavily favored. The engagement was fought in the presence of an estimated sixteen thousand spectators, who, "upon the heights of Cherbourg, the breakwater, and rigging of men-of-war, witnessed 'the last of the *Alabama.*' Among them were the captains, their families, and crews of two merchant ships burnt by the daring cruiser a few days before her arrival at Cherbourg, where they were landed in a nearly destitute condition."[31]

Captain Semmes, Captain Winslow and their officers became instant celebrities in Europe and at home. With so many eyewitnesses, the battle passed from news into poetry, song and numerous paintings, among them Edouard Manet's famous rendering of the battle climax. *Kearsarge* became an icon of American sea might and today is considered one of the three most important ships in the U.S. Navy.[32]

Long after she sank off the coast of Cherbourg, *Alabama* continued to haunt Fraser, Trenholm & Company. After the war, the United States sued Great Britain for damages done by warships built in Britain and sold to the Confederacy. Eight Confederate commerce raiders had captured or sank a total of 295 Union steamers, 44 large sailing ships and 683 schooners. Because of *Alabama*'s amazing interruption of maritime commerce, the suit was known as the Alabama Claims. (Commerce raiders destroyed half of the U.S. merchant fleet, and maritime commerce in the United States did not recover for eighty years.) International arbitration endorsed the American position, forcing Britain to pay the United States $15.5 million in 1872. It is speculated that the British government exchequered a Fraser, Trenholm & Company account and used the money to pay part of the fine.

In Charleston, litigation from George Trenholm's wartime pursuits dogged him until the end of his life and beyond. The federal government claimed that John Fraser and Company had illegally converted Confederate dollars into personal assets. It obtained the company's records and demanded import duty plus interest on everything that came through the blockade. To pay the taxes, the government sold the company's real estate assets at a fraction of their worth, for property values were severely depressed after the war.[33]

George Trenholm became ill in July 1875; his health continued to decline throughout the following year. In 1874, he was elected to the state House of Representatives, where he was considered one of the few respected white men who could work with the generally detested radical Reconstruction government. He lived just long enough to witness the election of General Wade Hampton as governor and died on December 9, 1876. Tributes to

Trenholm were numerous, including the flags of a hundred ships flying at half-mast in Charleston Harbor.

To settle the indebtedness of his estate, Trenholm's properties and those of his deceased partner, James Welsman, were auctioned off in April 1879. This included sale of 172 Rutledge Avenue, where Trenholm's wife, Anna Helen Holmes Trenholm, had lived for thirty-four years.[34] Banker Charles Otto Witte purchased the house, and in 1907, Witte's daughters sold 172 Rutledge Avenue to Mary Vardrine McBee, who founded Ashley Hall School for Girls on the property.

CHAPTER 8

Blockade Running

Running the blockade was a deadly cat-and-mouse game with high stakes. British investors alone spent an estimated £50,000 on runners, equivalent to some $2.5 billion in today's U.S. dollars. At the beginning of the war, a large portion of the ships managed to elude capture, but as the blockade became more effective, ordinary freighters were too slow to escape the increasingly vigilant, modern vessels being constructed for the Union Navy.

Investors quickly discovered that profits from long, transatlantic voyages did not justify the costs and began to ship fully-loaded, slower vessels across the ocean to intermediate points in Bermuda, Nassau and Havana where cargoes were reloaded into smaller vessels that dashed through the blockade.

These short runs required a new class of ships that could elude detection and hug the shoreline. Ship designers came up with a low-profile, shallow-draft, paddle-wheel steamer that was driven by powerful engines that burned smokeless anthracite coal. Built in the Liverpool area, the specialty vessels could achieve a speed of seventeen knots.

Blockade runners were manned primarily by British and European crews, interspersed with Confederate officers and coast pilots; pay was high. The ships' captains preferred to run at night, either on moonless nights or before the moon rose or after it set. When they approached the coast, they showed no lights, and sailors were prohibited from smoking. Union blockaders also covered their lights, except a faint light on the commander's ship. If a warship discovered a blockade runner, it fired rockets in the direction of its course. To confuse their pursuers, runners would also fire rockets in different directions.

U.S. fleet offshore. *Library of Congress.*

It is estimated that although about fifty percent of the runners got through, the blockade served as a deterrent for vessels who would have ordinarily conducted commerce in Confederate ports. In December 1865, Navy Secretary Wells reported that the Union Navy had captured or destroyed 1,022 vessels (295 blockade-running steamers, 44 sailing ships and 683 schooners); this did not included ships and cargo run ashore.[35]

THE CHARLESTON BLOCKADE

The blockade of Charleston started on May 11, 1861, with the frigate *Niagra*, a warship manned by six hundred sailors.

Those who had coffee, tea, and other commodities put them away for sickness and resorted to poorer beverages such as okra seeds that were parched a light brown and then ground. Plantation ladies made their own soaps, and a corncob burned to ashes in a clean Dutch oven became a substitute for corn starch. They boiled and refined myrtle berries to make candles, and learned to spin wool to knit stockings, mittens, and chest protectors for the soldiers. They learned how to make dyes from the forests, producing purples, yellows, crimsons, and browns. Ladies made wine, and replaced sugar with cane and sorghum syrup. Seawater was evaporated to make salt, a valuable commodity which children rolled and pulverized into table salt. In short, the Confederate households learned how to innovate to make something out of practically nothing.

Until the port was sealed, blockade runners came and went regularly. The famous Bee Store put on sale the entire cargo of each vessel as it came in; everything could be purchased with Confederate money. The Let Her Be and the Let Her Rip seemed to bear a charmed life. They were endeared to the childish heart by the very impudence of their names, while to the Chicora Company that owned them, they were little mines of wealth, bringing, besides, many comforts and necessaries to the people who toiled and the men who fought.[36]

Two daring brothers ran ships through the Charleston blockade. The more audacious was Captain Thomas Lockwood, whose exploits earned him almost legendary fame in his own lifetime.

Born in Smithville, near Wilmington, North Carolina, Tom Lockwood moved to Charleston when he was seventeen. He worked for the Florida Steam Packet Company, an ancillary of John Fraser and Company. Working his way up, Lockwood became captain of the *Carolina*, a side-wheel packet that transported mail, cargo and passengers between Charleston and Jacksonville. He married Anna McDougal in 1860 and purchased property in Charleston from his employer.

In July 1861, Lockwood received a commission as a Confederate privateer and began by capturing the *William McGilvery*. When privateering became increasingly difficult, his employer shifted Lockwood's services to running badly needed supplies into Southern ports.

In late 1861, President Jefferson Davis named commissioners James M. Mason and John Slidell to plead the Southern cause abroad. Southern newspapers foolishly announced that they would depart from Charleston on the Confederate raider *Nashville*, causing the North to double the number of blocking vessels outside the harbor entrance.

Once it was impossible for *Nashville* to depart, Tom Lockwood snooped around the harbor and noticed that *Gordon*, then up for sale, had escaped scrutiny. To acquire the boat for Confederate usage, John Fraser and Company offered to pay half of the charter money in exchange for return cargo space.

In October, under cover of a rainsquall, *Gordon* (renamed *Theodora*) slipped out of Charleston with Mason, Slidell, their families and aides aboard. The delayed departure caused them to miss their original rendezvous. Mason, Slidell and their entourage continued on to Cuba and took passage on the Royal Mail steamer *Trent*. Captain Charles Wilkes, commanding USS *San Jacinto*, waylaid *Trent* and removed the two men from the neutral English ship. Amid much nationalistic furor in the North, Mason and Slidell were incarcerated in Boston. This blatant abuse of English neutrality caused such an international crisis that it almost brought England to war against the North.

Thomas Lockwood. *Courtesy Robert Lockwood.*

Tom Lockwood's successful passage through the blockade made him a celebrity in Havana. He was wined and dined by Confederate expatriates and local sympathizers. Ladies gave him a Confederate ensign, which he promptly hoisted on his ship. The banner was still boldly flying when Lockwood entered Nassau Harbor. This brazen display of the Confederate symbol caused Union authorities to pressure British officials to force its removal. The irrepressible Lockwood promptly ordered the ensign nailed to the top of his mainmast, had the mast greased and dared anyone to remove it. And there it remained.

In December 1861, Robert Lockwood, Tom's brother, was in Nassau harbor aboard another Trenholm vessel. When the fully loaded *Gladiator* arrived from England without an assigned pilot, Robert helped guide the *Gladiator* into port. The British captain refused to leave port while Union ships lurked beyond the harbor entrance. Whereupon Trenholm firms worked behind-the-scenes and received permission to "break bulk" and transport the cargo piecemeal in smaller, faster ships, forever changing the delivery methods for British cargoes.

The timing was perfect. Tom Lockwood arrived aboard *Kate* (former *Carolina*) carrying cotton from Charleston. *Kate* and another ship were loaded with the *Gladiator*'s cargo, and the flamboyant Lockwood widely proclaimed to anyone who would listen that he planned to take *Kate* to Halifax. He departed and promptly ran the cargo into unguarded Mosquito Inlet, Florida.

Meanwhile, his brother Robert was given command of *Margaret and Jessie* in May 1862. While bringing supplies from Nassau, he boldly charged through the Charleston blockade at full speed while five blockaders shot at the ship, which amazingly, suffered little damage. *Margaret and Jessie* slipped back out of Charleston but pursuing Union ships forced her ashore on Eleuthera Island. After a controversy about claiming the prize money and the vessel's ownership, Trenholm agents regained control. Robert Lockwood made eighteen successful runs on *Margaret and Jessie* before he was captured outside of Wilmington in November 1863. The ship was confiscated and converted into USS *Gettysburg*; Robert Lockwood was imprisoned for the rest of the war.

Brother Tom fared better. Under his command, *Kate* became one of the most renowned packet steamers of the war. She would mingle among the Union ships by day flying a United States flag, and then steal away under the cover of darkness. Once she ran aground between an anchored man-of-war and breakers offshore. The blockaders did not see her, enabling the crew to jettison heavy coils of lead wire (bound to become Confederate bullets) and free the ship; the chief engineer loaded the safety valve down with iron castings to prevent noise from escaping and blew the steam off under water as *Kate* quietly escaped.

Lockwood's runs were so frequent and successful that he became a legend with friend and foe alike. *Kate* ran the blockade with lights darkened, and when near shore, she would display two lights on the shore side; shore lights would respond if it were safe to come in. Gideon Wells ordered Admiral DuPont, chief of the South Atlantic Blockading Squadron, to change the lineup outside of Charleston to a double line (inshore and offshore) after *Kate* brought in a steam engine for a ram being built in Charleston.

People in Wilmington, North Carolina, loved Lockwood because he was one of the first blockade runners to use that port. When anchored there, *Kate* was shot at by distant blockading vessels, and twice, federal expeditions attempted to destroy her at night.

Kate brought in four cargos before the bloody battle of Shiloh. After two successful runs to New Smyrna, Florida, in February 1862, Lockwood went to Charleston for his family. A Federal gunboat discovered *Kate*'s hiding place and forced her to flee to the Bahamas before Lockwood returned. The daring captain, his wife, their two children and a hired boy boarded a whaleboat and headed for Nassau. After surviving a terrible storm, the bedraggled group arrived in the open boat three weeks later.

Kate sank late in 1862 when she hit a snag in the Cape Fear River, after having made somewhere between twenty and forty runs and earning a fortune for Fraser, Trenholm & Company. Lockwood then was given command of *Atlantic* (later *Elizabeth*), which ran aground in September 1863.

Early 1864 found Tom Lockwood in Liverpool overseeing construction of two supersized blockade runners. By then Lockwood was known as "father of the trade" and insisted upon expensive special requirements for his new ship, *Colonel Lamb*. Lockwood's wife, Anna, christened the vessel, which was put into service in October 1864.

Colonel Lamb made successful runs into Nassau and Wilmington before the fall of Fort Fisher in January 1865. Once all the Atlantic Confederate ports were sealed, Lockwood had little to do and sailed to Halifax. Flying the Confederate ensign, he was giving a tour for the local citizenry when he learned of Lincoln's assassination. Lockwood promptly removed the offending banner out of respect for the fallen leader. Shortly thereafter, he returned *Colonel Lamb* to Fraser, Trenholm & Company in England.

Lockwood worked for the Florida Steam Packet line after the war and worked aboard *Kate*, the former blockade runner *Kate II* that had been retrofitted for passengers. Tom Lockwood died in Charleston in 1877.[37]

CHAPTER 9

Shipwrecked

The tightening blockade of Confederate ports became a bonanza for Liverpool shipbuilders. By 1864, ten new vessels had started to run the blockade with twenty others in progress. The majority was built by Jones, Quiggins & Company while other fine vessels were constructed at the shipyards of William C. Miller & Sons and W.H. Potter; on the other side of the Mersey River in Birkenhead were Laird Brothers and Bowdler & Chaffer.

William Cowley Miller got into Confederate shipbuilding when he was offered a tempting commission by the engineering works of Fawcett & Preston, a manufacturer of marine engines. His shipyard was on the banks of the Mersey River in Toxteth. A member of the Liverpool Council for South Toxteth, Miller was a highly respected citizen.

Miller had five sons: William Lodwick, Robert, Thomas, Henry and Edwin. William Lodwick didn't work in the company, and Robert was killed in a ship-launching accident when he was eighteen years old. At the time of the Civil War, Miller and sons Thomas, Henry and Edwin operated the shipyard. Thomas had inherited his father's drive and business acumen and was being groomed to take over the family business.

In addition to constructing the Confederate raider *Florida*, by 1864 the Miller shipyard had built the blockade runners *Let Her Be* (later *Chicora*), *Phantom* and *Mary Celestia*; *Lelia* was completed in January 1865; *Abigail* and *Ray* were launched in March 1865.[38] Two Miller-built blockade runners were commissioned by William G. Crenshaw & Company.

Tredegar Iron Works survived Richmond's evacuation conflagration because the owner, Joseph Anderson, reportedly paid over fifty armed guards to protect the facility from arsonists. Anderson had secured his assets overseas; he petitioned President Johnson for a pardon and was back in business almost immediately after the war. *Library of Congress.*

William Crenshaw was a part of a family considered the "merchant princes" of Richmond. Among their holdings was Crenshaw Woolen Mills, a factory sited near the Tredegar Iron Works. Originally a flour mill, it was converted to manufacture cloth used to make uniforms, blankets and stocking yarn for Confederate soldiers. Crenshaw products were said to be of superior quality to the ersatz "shoddy" woolen goods manufactured in Northern factories.

Crenshaw & Company also operated a small fleet of vessels, all named after female relatives of the firm's principles. After hostilities started, a number of blockade running vessels were added to the maritime operation. The North Atlantic Blockading Squadron lost no time in seizing Crenshaw ships. The schooner *Crenshaw* was captured by USS *Star* in 1861 and sold as a prize in New York; in 1862 while flying under a Union flag, *Crenshaw* was overtaken and burned by the Confederate commerce raider *Alabama*.

When Virginia seceded from the Union, William Crenshaw had raised and equipped at his own expense a battery of artillery known as Crenshaw's Battery. The battery fought in every battle from Cold Harbor to Sharpsburg.

As the war dragged on, the Confederate War Department realized that they had to counter the ever-increasing effects of the blockade and contracted with Crenshaw & Company to supplement official procurement facilities. Again, it was a family affair. Lewis D. Crenshaw remained in Richmond as head of the company's shipping interests and oversaw Crenshaw Woolen Mills until they were destroyed by fire in 1863; James R. Crenshaw managed the firm and set up offices in Charleston to procure cotton for blockade runners; Brother Joseph took charge of the offices in Wilmington, North Carolina, a principle port of entry. Captain Crenshaw left his beloved brigade and went to England with the dual purpose of purchasing needed commodities and contracting ships to run war materiel through the blockade.[39]

Crenshaw's first blockade running enterprise was a partnership with Alexander Collie & Company, but by early 1864, their ships had been lost, and the partnership folded. Operating under the name William G. Crenshaw & Company, Crenshaw independently set up his brother James as the agent who managed trade through Wilmington. This reciprocal trade arrangement converted cotton and sometimes tobacco into funds to purchase ordnance, clothing and provisions. Goods from England were shipped to the Confederacy via blockade runners from Bermuda and Nassau.

CSN Commander Arthur Sinclair of Norfolk, Virginia, and engineer Charles Francis Middleton of Charleston, South Carolina, chanced to be aboard the two Crenshaw paddlewheel steamers built by William C. Miller & Sons. With the convergence of their paths, they entered a world of foreign intrigue, daring chases and sensational shipwrecks. This is their story.

BLOCKADE RUNNER *MARY CELESTIA*

Launched in February 1864, *Mary Celestia* was described as a "rakish" 225-foot side-paddlewheel steamer. She successfully ran the blockade eight times. To confuse Union spies, there were aliases: *Bijou*, the name she was launched under; *Marie Celeste*; *Mary Celestia*; and *Mary Celeste*. (This blockade runner is not to be confused with the mystery ship *Mary Celeste*, the abandoned brigantine later popularized by Sir Arthur Conan Doyle.)[40]

After her delivery to Bermuda in early May 1864 under the command of W.G. Green,[41] *Mary Celestia* made her first run under the "Boy Captain" Michael P. Usina, who made a total of twenty-eight blockade runs during his career. He was twenty-four when he assumed command, making him the youngest captain in the blockade running fleet.[42] His chief engineer was John H. Sassard of Charleston, South Carolina.[43]

Captain Usina described *Mary Celestia*'s first run out of St. Georges, via Nassau, to Wilmington as uneventful. As Usina told the story years later, on the return voyage, she was spotted shortly after getting through the blockade. Poor visibility in a driving rain prevented seeing their pursuer until it was bearing down upon them. The seas were rough, and *Mary Celestia* was heavy laden. Suddenly, the larger ship came within easy gun distance.

To enable *Mary Celestia*'s bow to take the heavy seas more easily, Usina urged Engineer Sassard to take extreme measures to get more revolutions out of the engines and ordered forty-five forward bales of cotton (with the bands cut) thrown overboard. While their adversary sought to avoid the loose floating cotton, below deck Sassard put a lock on the safety valve and continued to apply steam to the boilers until the ship logged seventeen miles an hour in a heavy head sea. Fortunately, the untried English boilers did not fail, and *Mary Celestia* avoided capture or worse. Years later at a Confederate Veterans Reunion, Usina described Sassard as a brave, conscientious Christian gentleman seemingly with nerves of steel. (Official records show that this incident happened a month later.)[44]

On another run under Captain Usina, while en route from Nassau to Wilmington, yellow fever broke out. This was not unusual, for during the summer of 1864, the dreaded disease, called "yellow Jack," took many lives. Their pilot, John William (Billy) Anderson, was stricken shortly after they left Nassau and refused the captain's offer to return, wanting "to rest when they reached home." By the second day, Anderson was delirious, placing the ship in jeopardy for he was the only one aboard who was familiar with the treacherous New Inlet bar.

As *Mary Celestia* neared the North Carolina coast in the early light of dawn, a Union cruiser spotted her and took up the chase. Shells passed through the rigging and sent up columns of spray. Hearing the commotion, Anderson insisted upon being taken to the wheelhouse as the steamer raced for the protective guns of Fort Fisher. Everyone watched in awed silence as Anderson skillfully eased *Mary Celestia* safely across the bar. With the harbor in sight, Anderson bowed his head, and the horrified men saw him cough up black vomit, a sure sign that the end was near. *Mary Celestia* anchored in the bay off Smithville, and Captain Usina sent for Anderson's wife. Unfortunately, he passed away before she arrived.[45]

Instead of receiving a hero's welcome for bringing supplies through the blockade, *Mary Celestia* was quarantined offshore. Although only a few boats had the disease, communication with the shore was forbidden. Even attempted bribery did not work, and the men spent their time liming, fumigating and purifying the ship. (One hundred and fifty years ago, people did not realize that yellow fever was mosquito-borne.)

Chief Engineer Sassard left *Mary Celestia* with Captain Usina. He was replaced by thirty-three-year-old Assistant Engineer Charles F. (Charlie) Middleton, also of Charleston.

When hostilities started, records indicate that Captain C.F. Middleton, "an old resident of Sullivan's Island, remained with his family during the cannonade and was especially useful."[46] He joined the blockade running fleet sometime after James Crenshaw set up offices in Charleston in 1863. His letters mention leaving "little" *Caledonia*, a small blockade runner that ran a few times until captured (he was not on it then), and he wrote from *Robert E. Lee*, which was captured by *James Adger* on November 9, 1863. *Robert E. Lee*'s crew was sent with the ship to Boston for adjudication. Middleton was probably among them because he arrived in Bermuda on December 15, 1863, on the barque *Auctioneer*, from New York. That suggests he convinced the Yankees he was a British crewmember, and presumably, he was released on condition that he return to Britain. In an April 1864 letter, Middleton wrote that he had joined John Sassard in Bermuda awaiting *Florie*, although he later decided to join *Mary Celestia*.[47]

W.G. Green became the ship's master on the run from Wilmington in late June 1864. Apparently, Green had an altercation with Crenshaw and left. Green's replacement was Commander Arthur Sinclair (1810–1865), son of naval hero Arthur Sinclair (1780–1831), who fought in the War of 1812 and in the Barbary Pirate campaign.

Arthur Sinclair had followed his family's proud naval tradition. In 1852, he commanded *Supply* on Commodore Perry's history-making voyage to Japan; his son, another Arthur, was aboard as a midshipman and later served on the commerce raider *Alabama* while young Arthur's brother served on the equally infamous *Florida*.

The senior Arthur Sinclair and his two brothers resigned their U.S. commissions and joined the Confederate Navy in 1861. Arthur Sinclair first saw action in command of CSS *Winslow* at the Battle of Hatteras Inlet. As captain of the ill-fated ironclad CSS *Mississippi*, he ordered it burned to

Charles Francis Middleton. *Courtesy Philip A. Middleton.*

Sinking of *Mary Celestia*. Watercolor by Edward James, 1864. *Courtesy the National Museum of Bermuda.*

avoid capture when New Orleans fell in 1862. Sinclair was captain of the ironclad CSS *Atlanta* from February to May 1863. While posted in Richmond in 1864, he worked with marine scientists experimenting with mines and submarines. He was promoted to commander of *Squib* after it successfully exploded a primitive torpedo against USS *Minnesota*. He became captain of *Mary Celestia* in July 1864.

After what seemed like an eternity, *Mary Celestia* was permitted to make another run to Bermuda in late July; she made the return trip on Middleton's thirty-fourth birthday, August 3, 1864. This time, the little steamer was quarantined off Fort Anderson along with eight other boats. Again the ships had to unload their water barrels and leave them on the beach to be filled by soldiers who avoided all contact with the ships. The enforced isolation caused disciplinary problems with crewmembers.

Mary Celestia ran the blockade and delivered 683 bales of cotton to Bermuda on August 26. On September 6, she headed back to Wilmington with a cargo of 125 boxes of tinned meat and 534 boxes mysteriously labeled "merchandise." Piloted by an experienced Bermudian, John Virgin, she cleared Hamilton Harbor, made a fast run through the east end channel and eased toward land to permit the ship's owner and the pilot to disembark.

First Officer Stuart suddenly announced breakers ahead, to which Virgin replied, "I know every rock about here as well as I know my own house" and ignored the warning. The helmsman turned the wheel, but too late. Within seconds, the speeding vessel struck the reef and sank within eight minutes. The only life lost was that of the chief cook who went below to get a prized possession; the door slammed shut, taking him down with the sinking vessel. The cargo was floated out of the wreck as quickly as possible.

Confederate authorities demanded an explanation of how a boat could hit a reef in smooth water in broad daylight. They claimed that the U.S. consul to Bermuda, Charles Maxwell Allen, had bribed the pilot. Of course, he denied any involvement when he mentioned it in the September 26 Consular Records. Another explanation was that the accident was alcohol-fueled.[48]

Although the shipwreck was investigated by the Bermuda Pilot Commission and pilot Virgin was suspended from duty for several months, it was soon forgotten because of the necessities of war.

Today, *Mary Celestia* lies buried under the sands of an area known as the "Graveyard of the Atlantic." All that remains is a ghostly upright paddlewheel frame standing sentinel over the wreckage. Covered with white anemones, she is a veritable artificial reef teeming with marine life. Diving *Mary Celestia* has become one of Bermuda's most popular maritime attractions.

MAIDEN VOYAGE OF *LELIA*

Although most of *Mary Celestia*'s crew died of yellow fever while in Bermuda, Middleton, Captain Sinclair and the mate lived comfortably in the country awaiting another ship. Because the epidemic was causing blockade runners to avoid Bermuda, to save his life, Sinclair persuaded Middleton to join him on the blockade runner *Lelia*, still under construction in the shipyard of William C. Miller & Sons.

Middleton's last letter home in December 1864 indicates that they arrived in Liverpool safely and, upon inspection, found a sound ship. *Lelia*'s iron frame was covered with an overlapping steel-plate skin. To drive the powerful paddlewheels, she was equipped with twin Fawcett & Preston steam engines. At full speed, the engines required almost fifty tons of coal a day. For the voyage across the Atlantic, the main and after holds had been filled with extra coal, with a total amount of 460 tons aboard.

Crenshaw took great care to ensure *Lelia* did not violate any British neutrality laws. Put in command was an experienced blockade runner, Virginian Thomas Buxton Skinner, age thirty-eight. The crew was mostly British.

Arthur Sinclair was registered as a passenger, not as a Confederate officer; he was slated to take command when *Lelia* reached Bermuda. To honor the distinguished captain, William Crenshaw followed his custom and named the vessel after Sinclair's wife, Lelia. Sinclair had purchased a watch made by Robert Roskell of Liverpool for £40; Crenshaw's manager had presented Sinclair with a gold watch chain complete with a mariner's compass and locket containing a lock of Lelia Sinclair's hair. Someone suggested that Sinclair leave the watch behind for safekeeping, but he decided to take it with him to purchase food and shelter in the event of capture. He also deposited more than £1,300 gold with Crenshaw & Company, stipulating that in the event of his death, £100 was to go to each of his sons and the remainder to his wife.

Lelia set sail on January 14. It is speculated that she left Liverpool in a hurry because it was believed that Northern interests would somehow stop her from sailing. Aboard were forty-five officers and crew, plus six listed passengers. In addition there was Thomas Miller, *de facto* head of the family, who was to be put ashore at Holyhead, along with two pilots and a shipping clerk with Crenshaw & Company. [49]

The shipwreck was a classic tragedy. In January 1865, northwesterly gales had been battering the west coast of England for a week. Although the barometer was ominously low, no storm warning had been hoisted. Lulled into a false sense of security, at half past nine that fateful Saturday morning, *Lelia* proceeded down the Mersey at full speed. The ship was heavy laden and low in the water.

About noon, *Lelia* left the sheltered waters at the river's mouth and entered Liverpool Bay near the coast of Wales. The wind suddenly picked up, and she encountered the full force of a fierce winter storm. The vessel pitched and rolled as huge waves unrelentingly crashed onto the deck.

Unprepared for the heavy seas, Captain Skinner ordered that the vessel be slowed and the anchors secured; they were stowed with the fluke over the rail and the crown on the deck. This prevented the forward hatches from being closed. Water continued to smash onto the deck faster than it rolled off, eventually swamping the crew's quarters.

The struggling *Lelia* took four hours to reach Great Orme's Head. Captain Skinner decided to turn back and hoisted a distress signal. The *Sovereign*, a steamer bound for Bristol, noticed the signal, altered her course and followed *Lelia* until it determined that she could not catch up with the speeding vessel. Sadly, *Sovereign* turned away too soon.

It was reported later that a huge wave lifted one of the anchors and smashed the fluke through the deck. Another wave washed away the iron covering of a scuttle, and the water began pouring into the bow. Through a series of mishaps, the crew could not access the equipment necessary to pump out the vessel, and the deck soon sank to the level of the raging sea.[50] The official finding was that the crew apparently forgot to fit the hawse pipe covers after weighing anchor. Plowing through the turbulent waves, water was forced into *Lelia*'s hawse pipes, down into the chain locker and into the forward hold. (Anchor chains pass through hawse pipes and should have close-fitting covers or plugs to stop water from entering a vessel.)

At one point, the lifeboats were slung out, only for Commander Sinclair to order them to be re-stowed.

Once it became obvious that *Lelia* could not be saved, Captain Skinner gave orders to abandon ship. As the bow began to sink, the men crowded onto the stern waiting to board lifeboats. Two got tangled in the rigging and were useless before they could be lowered into the water. The crew and passengers who managed to get into the remaining lifeboats met catastrophe and capsized before reaching the Mersey River Lightship, about one-and-a-half miles distant. Only twelve freezing and exhausted survivors were eventually pulled out of the sea at the Northwest Lightship.

A rescue effort manned by the Liverpool Lifeboats also met calamity, and seven men who had refused to don their cumbersome life jackets drowned when their boat capsized as they were being towed in the storm-tossed waters.

Heroic Captain Skinner went down with his ship in spite of the fact that he had an opportunity to board the last lifeboat that made it to the water. His last act was to fire up distress rockets.

Although many ships went down off the English coast during that January storm, the sensational wreck of *Lelia* received the most attention. The shipwreck was thoroughly investigated by the Board of Trade in Liverpool.

In time, *Lelia*'s sad fate faded from the news, that is, until what remained of a man, still fully dressed in an overcoat and uniform, was pulled from the sea four months later. The body was positively identified as Arthur Sinclair because of the ornate gold watch still in his pocket. The watch had stopped at 4:10 p.m., providing the time Sinclair was thrown into the sea.

The consequences of the shipwreck were far reaching. The families of the lifeboat rescuers were left without their breadwinners. For the Miller

Lifeboat overturned en route to rescue the crew of the *Lelia*. From contemporary publication.

family, the shipwreck was equally devastating. The adverse effects of the commercial raiders had made it difficult for the Miller shipyard to continue building warships for the Confederates; Union spies and court proceedings caused the gunboat CSS *Alexandra* to be seized before delivery. William Miller's health began to deteriorate after his son Thomas did not return, and he died in 1869.[51] The Miller shipyard closed the following year.

Arthur Sinclair Jr., who had been rescued by the English yacht *Deerhound* after the Battle of Cherbourg, met with his father before *Lelia* left Liverpool. George Terry Sinclair, his younger brother, had been aboard *Florida* when she was captured in neutral Bahia, Brazil. After a time as a prisoner of war, he was paroled and had made his way to Liverpool. Both sons attended Sinclair's funeral at Fleetwood Cemetery. Arthur Sinclair's wife had been cruelly evicted from her home in Norfolk when the city was captured by Union forces. She, too, traveled to England to claim her inheritance. (In a curious footnote to history, Arthur Sinclair's great-grandson was Upton Sinclair, the prolific twentieth-century author and social activist.)

In time, Middleton's wife realized that her husband wasn't coming home and struggled to support her young family by opening a millinery shop in Charleston with her last assets, about $3,000 in gold. (As a precaution against capture, before leaving for Bermuda, Middleton had deposited a gold watch and chain given to him by Billy Anderson, a breast pin and a belt containing

Capture of Fort Fisher, Kurz and Allison. *Library of Congress.*

$600 of gold coins with his employer.) Knowing little about business, she lost her little capital.[52]

The tragic attempt to put *Lelia* in blockade running service was in vain. Mighty Fort Fisher, guardian of the last major Confederate port, fell the day after *Lelia* sank.

In 1996, amateur diver Chris Michael, head of Theoretical Physics at Liverpool University, used a magnetometer to locate what he thought to be remains of *Lelia*. Later he dived the wreck and discovered a bronze bell inscribed "LELIA 1864." This find led him to research and publish *Lelia* in 2004. Michael theorized: "With many experienced officers aboard they may have been over-complacent…There was a design weakness in blockade runners. They were built to be very low in the water to evade detection and travel across shallow seas…Once you get an ingress of water into the bow, the ship noses down into the waves and is finished."[53]

CHAPTER 10

Charleston

1861

Before the Revolution, one of the causes of colonial dissatisfaction was the British practice of quartering troops within the civilian population. In reaction, in May 1792, the new Congress established a national defense system based on individual state militias that were required to serve only in times of emergency.

South Carolina's defense system was based on this act. By 1841, the state's militia was comprised of two divisions of infantry troops that were broken down into nine battalions. Each battalion had five companies of roughly thirty to sixty-four officers and enlisted men. There were also elite "volunteer" companies of men who had the means to purchase uniforms, rifles, artillery and horses. According to the law, all white males between the ages of sixteen and sixty could be required to serve in some capacity and those between eighteen and forty-five could be activated for three months inside the state and for two months outside of South Carolina.

Because of the costs involved, by 1860 many companies throughout the state had disbanded or had become little more than social clubs.

Charleston was different. The bastion of Lowcountry aristocracy, it had a population of over forty thousand and boasted the best-equipped unit in the state, the Fourth Brigade. Under the command of Brigadier General Wilmot G. DeSaussure, it included the First Regiment of Rifles with seven companies, under Colonel J.J. Pettigrew; the Seventeenth Regiment, under Colonel John Cunningham, with ten companies; and four rifle companies manned by the

Southern Military Academy at Marion Square. *Library of Congress.*

city's volunteer fire departments. The Charlestonians were proud of their uniforms and delighted in parading whenever the occasion arose.[54]

After the Denmark Vesey slave rebellion in 1822, South Carolina established a municipal guard composed of 150 men. Twenty years later, the legislature established the South Carolina Military Academy and passed an act to convert the existing state citadel located north of Boundary (later Calhoun) Street into the South Carolina Military Academy. The first twenty cadets reported to the academy in the spring of 1843.

The South Carolina Military Academy was incorporated into the state's military organization after secession. Known as the Battalion of State Cadets, their primary duties were mounting and manning heavy guns, guard duty, security and escorting prisoners. Cadets served in and around Charleston and helped defend the Charleston and Savannah Railroad at Tulifinny Creek when the Confederate troops forced the Union to withdraw in December 1864. The school ceased operation when Union troops entered the city in February 1865. Of the 224 Citadel alumni living at the time of the Civil War, 209 served in combat, mostly in the Confederate Army, where forty-nine died of combat wounds, several were wounded in action and many became prisoners of war.

LINCOLN'S CALL TO ARMS

On April 15, immediately after the surrender of Fort Sumter, President Lincoln issued a proclamation asking the militias of the states still in the Union to supply seventy-five thousand troops for ninety days' duration

Lieutenant General Robert E. Lee, CSA. *Library of Congress.*

to "repossess the forts, places, and property which have been seized from the Union, and in every event the utmost care will be observed…to avoid any devastation, any destruction of or interference with property, or any disturbance of peaceful citizens in any part of the country."

Northerners, outraged by the attack on Fort Sumter, immediately answered Lincoln's call. In fact, so many volunteered that some states oversubscribed their quotas.

Down South, the reaction was different. Although still in the Union, the "Border States" declared that they would not send volunteers to subjugate their brethren in South Carolina, Georgia, Alabama, Florida, Mississippi, Louisiana and Texas.

Virginia was the key border state. Their quota was three regiments or 2,340 men. The governor of Virginia refused to send troops and mobilized the state militia. The Virginia legislature had voted down secession on April 4. After Lincoln's request, however, on April 17 the legislature authorized secession contingent upon ratification by a statewide referendum. During the convention, former governor Henry Wise announced that capture of the arsenal at Harpers Ferry and the Gosport Navy Yard in Norfolk were already in progress.

On April 18, the Harpers Ferry arsenal was captured and most of the machinery was moved to Richmond. Fearing attack, the Union navy hastily abandoned Norfolk and the navy yard, torching as much as possible. Colonel Robert E. Lee resigned his army commission and joined the Confederate forces.

Following the Virginia legislature's vote for secession, Lincoln called for forty-two thousand three-year volunteers and ordered a blockade of all Southern ports.

After that, things rapidly deteriorated. Arkansas joined the Confederacy on May 6. Although Tennessee had rejected secession in February, once Lincoln called for more volunteers, Tennessee adopted a resolution to dissolve their ties with the Union on May 6 and confirmed secession by a referendum in June. On May 20, North Carolina voted unanimously to join the Confederacy. The following day, the Confederate Congress voted to move the capital from Montgomery, Alabama, to Richmond, Virginia. When the citizens from eastern Virginia ratified secession, the western part of the state broke with the eastern part of the commonwealth.

Meanwhile, across the ocean, the Confederacy's hopes for sovereign recognition were dashed May 13 when Great Britain declared neutrality.

Virginian voters ratified the articles of secession on May 23, 1861, but the results were held in secret for a couple of days in order to give the state time to secure their defenses. After notification of the election results, Colonel Thomas J. (later "Stonewall") Jackson shut down the Baltimore and Ohio Railroad. The following day, the Union army crossed the Potomac, seized Arlington, the home of Robert E. Lee, and captured Alexandria without a fight.

CHARLESTONIANS AT MANASSAS

Eager to "kill a Yankee" before hostilities ended, volunteer troops from South Carolina hastened to northern Virginia. Charleston volunteers were the first to face Northern forces. They were given the honor of forming the first brigade of the first division of the first "Confederate" troops in Northern Virginia. In fact, so many soldiers headed north (approximately six thousand) that Governor Pickens forbade more Charleston companies from leaving the region.

The first major battle of the war occurred on July 21 when Union forces attempted to take control of the railroad junction at Manassas. After the battle (called Bull Run by a Northern naming convention), Charleston witnessed its first military funeral when the bodies of the dead were shipped back home. The caskets were escorted to city hall and draped in black. Among the deceased were local heroes Lieutenant Colonel Benjamin A. Johnson,[55] second in command of the Hampton Legion, and Brigadier General Barnard Elliott Bee.

Bee had become a national hero. Not only had he ordered artillery fire that checked the first Union advance, he attained immortality while rallying his men. "Look at Jackson's brigade," he shouted. "It stands there like a stone wall." Bee was mortally wounded in the second Confederate charge, and his death was mourned throughout the South. General Bee's casket was escorted to St. Paul's Episcopal Church with an honor guard of the Charleston Riflemen and the Washington Light Infantry, with the entire Seventeenth Regiment following.

The Charleston Riflemen and Charleston Mounted Guard escorted Francis Bartow's casket to the Savannah Railroad Station for shipment back to Georgia. Bartow was the first Confederate brigade commander to die in combat. Only eight months earlier, Bartow's oratory had mesmerized the huge secession meeting at Institute Hall. Now he was heroically dead. (After his horse had been killed, Bartow had grabbed a fallen Confederate's horse and charged again, this time right into a Yankee bullet. As he lay dying, he shouted to his men, "They have killed me, but never give up this field." His regiment was practically annihilated during the battle.)

PORT ROYAL FALLS

In 1861, things were not going well for the Union forces. After the loss of Fort Sumter, they had suffered the disastrous defeat at Manassas in July and another at Ball's Bluff in October. The blockade was proving ineffectual, and Lincoln needed a decisive victory to boost the nation's morale. He moved swiftly.

The Union army needed a staging area for its troops, and the South Atlantic Blocking Squadron needed a southern deepwater port to supply its vessels. Although Hatteras Inlet had been captured, it was not large enough to accommodate the massive influx of men and materiel required for the war effort. Port Royal Sound had the deepest harbor south of New York City and was the obvious choice. Midway between Charleston and Savannah, it also provided an ideal location to combat blockade runners.

The strategic objective was to establish winter quarters on Hilton Head Island and to capture one or more southern ports. Lincoln appointed General Thomas Sherman (known as the "other Sherman") to organize twelve thousand troops; Commodore Samuel Francis DuPont was tasked with preparing the naval expedition.

Called the grandest armada in American history, a mighty fleet sailed out of Hampton Roads, Virginia, on October 29. In addition to 18 warships, supply ships carried troops, 1,500 tons of ordnance, hundreds of thousands of gallons of water, 2,000 bushels of coal, 1,500 horses and 8,000 bags of oats, in addition to miscellaneous wagons and professional drivers, building materials and 1,000 black laborers.

Although the War Department tried to keep the destination of the invasion secret until the fleet sailed, news about the invasion spread quickly. When boats were spotted along the coast, General DeSaussure, commander of the Fourth Brigade, issued orders to equip the 864 men of the Seventeenth Regiment for the attack everyone knew was coming.

General Beauregard had recognized the military value of Port Royal Sound and had ordered two forts to be hastily built to guard the expansive harbor: Fort Beauregard on Bay Point and Fort Walker on Hilton Head Island. In command of Confederate defenses was Brigadier General

The naval expedition to Beaufort (*Harpers Weekly*, November 30, 1861.) *Library of Congress.*

Thomas Fenwick Drayton, who had been appointed by Jefferson Davis, his former classmate at West Point.

Many locals were paralyzed by disbelief that the Yankees could win and stayed to watch as eighteen warships with two hundred mounted guns and fifty-five supporting craft appeared off Port Royal Sound. On November 3, the rector of St. Helena's Episcopal Church advised his congregation to evacuate, and on November 4, General Ripley urged the citizens to leave Beaufort immediately.

On November 8, in spite of determined resistance, the combined Confederate sea and land defenses did not have the firepower to stop the warships. By mid-afternoon, both forts had fallen, forcing the Confederates to hastily withdraw. Casualties were light on both sides.

During the engagement, Thomas Drayton had faced his brother Percival Drayton commanding the *Pocahontas*. According to family tradition, before the war, the brothers had met at St. Michael's Church, prayed for God's guidance, shook hands and departed to fulfill their separate destinies.[56]

General Sherman lost no time in landing troops to establish a southern base of operations. Pillaging was rampant. Union troops joined the slaves in looting the vacant plantations until Sherman ordered it stopped.

Union forces erecting a pontoon bridge in Beaufort, South Carolina. *Library of Congress.*

The sudden loss of Port Royal was a terrible military reversal for the Confederates. The next day, the government in Richmond sent Robert E. Lee to command South Carolina, Georgia and eastern Florida troops.

Lee had yet to make his reputation, and many did not consider him able to conduct a vigorous defense of Charleston and Savannah. Governor Pickens disagreed and wrote Jefferson Davis that he had "a very high estimation of his [Lee's] science, patriotism and enlightened judgment. I am also delighted with his high bred cultivated bearing. If he has a fault it is over caution, which results from his scientific mind."[57]

Families were forced to abandon their homes after the fall of Port Royal. View of Beaufort from the waterfront, December 1861. *Library of Congress.*

Lee reorganized the entire coastal defense system. He placed his headquarters at Coosawhatchie on the line of the Charleston and Savannah Railroad. Lee's strategy was to obstruct waterways between Charleston and Savannah that were not already in Union control and to protect the railroad so that his troops could be mobile. Lee conceded that the islands on the South Carolina coast were not defensible. He appointed General Roswell Ripley over the Charleston district.

Governor Pickens informed Lee that of the 2,700 infantry, artillery and cavalry left to defend the coast, only 1,531 officers and men were actually available for combat. These men were deployed at posts around Charleston. In response to this new threat so close to home, companies from the city's militia were posted on Wadmalaw Island and Johns Island.

Things were desperate around Port Royal Sound. Totally unprepared for the Confederate debacle, entire families made hasty exits from Beaufort, Edisto, St. Helena and other Sea Islands, some fleeing so unexpectedly that they left all their household effects behind.

Through the unique communication channels known only to slaves, once they learned of the Union victory, they refused to accompany their

Port Royal Island. Preparing cotton for the gin on Smith's plantation. *Library of Congress.*

departing masters. Ironically, 1861 had yielded a bumper cotton crop and the rewards had promised to be enormous. The profit-minded planters had reluctantly "volunteered" their slaves to construct the two forts protecting Port Royal; now they were forced to burn their precious cotton to prevent it from falling into enemy hands. The fires' glow eerily illuminated the seacoast for miles around.

Many plantation refugees came to Charleston. The city was already crowded with soldiers, and the displaced were forced to trade spacious mansions for cramped empty boxcars. Their plight was such that they were grateful for the makeshift accommodations. Charlestonians felt very sympathetic toward them, not realizing that many would soon share their same sad fate.

The Great Fire of 1861

For many years, a fire watchman had been posted in St. Michael's steeple. His job was to hang a red lantern if he observed smoke or signs of fire. The night of December 11 was warm and pleasant for that time of year. Suddenly, Charleston residents spotted the ominous red lantern, a grim portent of things to come.

The disaster started innocently enough. A seemingly unimportant fire broke out in Ruzel & Co.'s window and sash factory at East Bay and Hasell Streets. As the wind picked up, the fire quickly crossed the street to Cameron & Company's machine shops. By the time news spread, wind-fanned flames were already heading in a southwesterly course across Ansonborough, down Meeting Street and making a path between Queen and Broad Streets.

Twenty-two engines and eleven companies responded to the fire that night, but with many of their experienced firefighters in uniform, ranks had been greatly reduced. (In 1861, the South Carolina Assembly had exempted Charleston's firemen from military service, but in spite of this, many firefighters were among the first to volunteer.) To make matters worse, with so many men away, the tidal drains that supplied water were clogged due to lack of maintenance.

Fearing that a new steam fire engine would destroy the *esprit de corps* of the volunteers, Fire Chief Moses Henry Nathan and the board of firemasters had lobbied against the city's using them in Charleston's Volunteer Fire Department. (Mid-nineteenth century volunteer firefighters had traditionally used hand-pump fire engines and often sang to keep time as they pumped.) During the fire, the controversial steam pump was put into service and helped compensate for the reduced manpower.

The Pinckney house at East Bay and Market Streets was one of the first to go. Luckily, its contents and elderly Harriott Pinckney were saved by a relative, Captain John Rutledge, and the crew of the *Lady Davis*. Rutledge took her to his Tradd Street residence, but it, too, soon succumbed to the flames.

General Ripley's men were able to quell the flames at the Catholic Orphan House, but nobody could save St. John's and St. Finbar's

Above: Ruins of the Pinckney house. *Courtesy the College of Charleston Special Collections Library, Waddell collection, Charleston, South Carolina.*

Opposite top: Meeting Street seen from the roof of the Mills House; ruins of the Circular Church and Institute Hall south of the church. *Library of Congress.*

Opposite bottom: Broad Street: left, St. John's and St. Finbar's Roman Catholic Cathedral; center, St. Andrew's Hall; right, Dr. Gadsden's house, which was damaged during the bombardment of Charleston. It took thirty years to raise funds to build a new cathedral over the foundation of St. John's and St. Finbar's; St. Andrew's Hall was later demolished. *Library of Congress.*

Cathedral nearby. Located on the corner of Broad and Legare Streets, it had been completed only eight years earlier. A showplace, it was crowned with a gold cross that stood 285 feet in the air. The *Charleston Courier* wrote its obituary: "All of a sudden it was announced that beautiful architectural structure, St. John's and St. Finbar's Cathedral was in flames. The pride of that portion of our city was doomed to destruction, and its beautiful spire soon fell with a terrific crash, sounding high above the noise of the devouring flames." Residents living near the cathedral had believed it was fireproof and moved their belongings into the church. But all was

lost, for the cathedral's insurance policy had expired the week before the fire and had not yet been renewed.

Robert E. Lee and his staff had climbed to the roof of the Mills House to witness the devastating inferno. When they returned to the hotel's parlor, they found a group of ladies and their babies preparing to leave. Lee took one baby and another officer took the other, and they hastily exited through the cellar into the smoky chaos outside. Lee and his men were taken to the house of Charles Alston at 21 East Battery. Miraculously, the Mills House was saved by the staff who used wet blankets to smother the sparks and embers that blew onto the roof and window ledges.[58]

The fire continued to burn until it ran out of fuel near the Ashley River. Throughout the pandemonium, vehicles of every description carried away the effects of those fleeing the southwestern part of the city.

By the next day, dire tales circulated about the homeless and the loss of Charleston's iconic buildings: Institute Hall on Meeting Street, the Charleston Theatre on King Street and St. Andrew's Hall on Broad. Five churches and six hundred private homes were also destroyed. Although no lives were lost, real estate losses were staggering. The fire had consumed 145 acres with estimated damages of $7 million. The overwhelming destruction forced all but one insurance company into bankruptcy.[59]

Most of the working people lost everything, causing thousands to roam the streets. Children from the Orphan House were billeted above Aimar's Drug Store at King and Wentworth Streets; the German Friendly Society donated its building to students who had lost their school. Mayor Charles Macbeth asked those who had not lost property to donate food, clothing and shelter to those who were displaced. The response was heartening. A relief center was set up at the Confederate courthouse, and area planters donated food. Some military companies donated their pay to alleviate the suffering. An extra train loaded with supplies arrived from Augusta. In the confusion, the overtaxed military advised the removal of homeless noncombatants from Charleston, although only a few left.[60]

By Christmastime, needs in the city were so great that Lee was dismayed to find only 310 of General DeSassaure's troops were actually on duty. Many had gone home to spend Christmas with their families; others had wanted to do what they could to help after the catastrophic fire.[61]

Where aid from across the nation had poured into Charleston after the disastrous fire of 1837, the mood in the North was different now. The *New York Herald* commented that the fire must have been divine retribution and expressed the hope that it was an omen that foretold ruin of the rebellion.

The article described the devastation caustically:

> *Institute Hall—where the Democratic Convention was held, which split the party and split the nation; the theatre—to which the secessionists retired to hold a separate convention; the Charleston Hotel and the Mills House—where the warring factions respectively held their headquarters; St. Andrew's Hall—where the secession ordinance was passed; the cannon and ammunition foundries, the treason shops of the Mercury and Courier, and the headquarters of Governor Pickens—have all been laid in ashes.*

The December 28 *Harper's Weekly* opined that "Whatever the politicians and the papers may say, the Southern people from Norfolk to Galveston are sure to conclude that the negroes did the dread deed, and each man and woman is now quaking in terror lest his or her house should be the next to go."

Locals knew better. According to Lizzie Frost, "A good many persons think [the fire] was helped by the negroes and some think Yankee emissaries, but the fire took a very natural direction, following the course of the wind entirely—most of the negroes behaved admirably, our own servants and those of the neighborhood were untiring in their efforts to save everything, and to do all they could for us." [62] (The fire's origins are thought to have been caused by a cookfire in a vacant lot that was used by slaves who accompanied the Sea Island refugees.)

In the aftermath of the fire, Fire Chief Nathan established a fire-alarm telegraph system that helped firefighters locate fires more accurately. This eliminated the need for a watchman in St. Michael's steeple. (This was the fifth fire-telegraph system in the nation. It became a casualty of war that was not reestablished until Reconstruction.)

Some years later, a reflective Chief Nathan wrote: "It would seem that the hand of Providence intended this misfortune, for had not the fire happened many lives would have been lost in the bombardment of the city by the cursed Yankees, for thousands of their shells fell harmlessly in the burnt district which otherwise would have fell into the homes but for the fire." [63]

Today it is recognized that with so many white volunteer firefighters bearing arms, it was the free blacks who put out the fires caused by the Union bombardment during the siege and saved Charleston's remaining buildings from utter destruction.

CHAPTER II

The Lull Before the Storm
1862

B y February 1862, it was obvious that the war was going to last longer than originally anticipated, and the Confederate government demanded more troops from South Carolina. As the volunteer militia companies were due to muster out that month, state authorities appealed to the one-year volunteers in Virginia to reenlist and announced that on March 20, all eligible males between the ages of eighteen and forty-five would be conscripted.

There was an immediate call for more volunteers to man Charleston's local defenses. General Wilmot G. DeSaussure, retiring commander of the Fourth Brigade, exhorted citizens to volunteer, and loyal Charlestonians responded. New companies were formed, and the old companies split as volunteers filled the ranks of twelve companies.

The name Charleston Battalion first appeared in the *Charleston Mercury* at the end of February. By April 15, the new battalion consisted of the Charleston Riflemen, Charleston Light Infantry, Irish Volunteers, Sumter Guards, Calhoun Guards, Union Light Infantry and German Fusiliers.

The battalion volunteers were generally regarded above other regiments in both social position and education. Representing all ethnic groups in the city, they came from the professions, merchants, trades, shops, etc. The total number of men was 558, with 33 black Charlestonians, 24 of whom were listed as cooks and 8 as musicians or drummers who also filled the dangerous dual role of stretcher-bearers. Although men from other parts of the state were justifiably proud to have served in the battalion, Charleston names like Allston, Blake, Buist, Chisholm, Elliott, Frost, Guignard, Hayne, Huguenin,

Lowndes, MacGrath, Muckenfuss, Palmer, Ramsay, Rhett, Riley, Ryan, Seabrook, Simons, Trenholm and Waring dominated the roster.

General Johnson Hagood later described them as "not equal to some others in…discipline, but under his command would go anywhere and do anything… There was too much intelligence and too little rigidity of discipline in [the] ranks for men without force of character to command it successfully."[64]

Before Robert E. Lee left in March 1862, he placed General Roswell S. Ripley in command of the Charleston district. By then, life in the city had started to decline. Due to the blockade, stores had gradually closed, and gambling saloons sprang up to entertain the soldiers, much to the disgust of the local residents who remained.

On April 15, the Charleston Battalion was deployed to James Island under the command of Lieutenant Colonel Peter Gaillard and Major J.M. Harleston; they encamped near the fortification on the Secessionville peninsula. The following day, the Confederate government in Richmond passed a national conscription act that made every able-bodied Southern male between eighteen and thirty-five eligible for compulsory military service for three years or until the end of the war, whichever came first. In spite of the fact that they were locked in for the duration, there was enormous esprit de corps among those who served in the Charleston Battalion.[65]

SMALLS'S DARING ESCAPE

After the fall of Fort Sumter, things remained relatively calm in Charleston until an enslaved river pilot commandeered the *Planter* and made a daring dash for freedom. The *Planter* was a three-hundred-ton side-wheel commercial steamship that had been pressed into service by the Confederate army. With civilian Captain C.J. Relyea at the helm, she became General Ripley's flagship and was used as a dispatch boat to transport Confederate troops, inspect the forts and chart the actions of the enemy.

Captain Relyea always wore a straw hat. One day, as a joke, a slave put the hat on the head of Robert Smalls,[66] the ship's pilot. Someone told Smalls that he looked just like the captain. Smalls had planned to buy his freedom and that of his family, but the comment caused him to plot a more daring way out of bondage.

On May 13, *Planter* took aboard several large guns; afterward, Captain Relyea and the white officers went ashore for the evening, leaving Smalls in charge. With the officers absent, the crew slipped *Planter* from its mooring at 40 East Bay Street

Robert Smalls. (May 1862 *Harper's Weekly.*) *Library of Congress.*

and picked up family members who had been hiding at a nearby dock. Smalls disguised himself by putting on Relyea's straw hat and made an audacious run past the unsuspecting Confederate forts guarding the harbor.

Smalls's escape had major consequences for both sides. In addition to artillery pieces and ordinance, *Planter* carried a code book containing secret signals and the placement of mines in Charleston harbor. Smalls provided Admiral DuPont detailed information about the harbor's defenses and news that the Confederates had abandoned Folly Island and Coles Island, both barrier islands that guarded the Stono River. DuPont ordered several gunboats to investigate and, in practically no time, Union soldiers had established a base of operations on Folly Island.[67]

"Bird's-eye view of the city of Charleston, South Carolina, showing the approaches of Union gunboats." (*Harper's Weekly*, July 5, 1862.) *Courtesy Charleston Museum, Charleston, South Carolina.*

Farther south, Small's intelligence convinced Major General David Hunter, who had recently replaced Thomas Sherman, that this was an opportune time to capture Charleston. Hunter's strategy was to work his way up to the mouth of the Stono River and capture Fort Johnson, a key fortification protecting Charleston Harbor. He hastily assembled two divisions and headed north.

With the increased Union activity nearby, martial law was declared in Charleston, making the city little more than an armed camp. General Nathan "Shanks" Evans, hero of Manassas, hastily arrived to take charge of the James Island defenses. With almost certain conflict looming on the horizon, many of Charleston's inhabitants began fleeing the city in panic.

SECESSIONVILLE

In early June, under the protection of Union gunboats, 6,300 men landed on Grimball's plantation at the southwestern end of James Island. Although there was light resistance, General Hunter decided that he needed more troops before taking action. He placed Brigadier General Henry W. Benham in charge, giving him strict orders not to advance without instructions from headquarters.

With the increased enemy presence, the commander of the Confederate forces redeployed three batteries to James Island and ordered buildup of the earthwork defenses protecting approaches to the island. One of these fortifications was the tower fort at Secessionville, with 750 troops under the command of Colonel T.G. Lamar.

Shaped like the letter "M," the fort was bordered on each side by marsh. It was defended by nine canons; two twenty-four-pounders at a flanking battery had not yet received their gun crews. Two hours' march away, three regiments of Confederate infantry (two thousand) were waiting in reserve to support any action on the island.

On the night of June 15, General Benham decided to make an unauthorized "reconnaissance in force" on the Secessionville fort. Benham planned a surprise frontal assault before daybreak, attacking in two waves. Marched at double time, 3,500 troops struggled across unfamiliar terrain. Navigating two hedgerows and a weed-choked cotton field in the dark caused the men to break formation. Some troops bogged down in the marshes. The rest were compressed in the center, slowing the advance to the extent that the second wave ran into the first.

That same evening, Colonel Lamar had kept his men working until 4:00 a.m. The exhausted Confederate defenders were suddenly alerted when Union soldiers encountered their pickets about 5:00 a.m. Forewarned, Colonel Lamar mounted the parapet and observed the Union front about seven hundred yards away and moving.

By the time the Confederates assembled and began shooting, the advancing troops were scarcely two hundred yards distant. Lamar dispatched a request for emergency reinforcements and took charge of the center canon, tearing a great hole in the advancing lines with a barrage of grapeshot, nails, iron chain and glass. The Seventy-ninth New York kept coming and mounted the parapet. They were engaged in hand-to-hand combat with the defenders until Union artillery opened fire on the fort and forced them to withdraw. The retreating men hampered the second wave from attacking.

At the same time, the Third New Hampshire and Third Rhode Island were attempting a flanking maneuver that brought them within several yards of the fort. Pluff mud and water impeded their crossing so they shot across the marsh, driving the defenders from the parapets.

During the assault, the two twenty-four-pounders on the right flank were silent. Colonel Ellison Capers of the Twenty-fourth South Carolina Infantry went to investigate and found that the gun crews had arrived but had never been trained. Capers started loading and firing at the enemy as he taught the men to shoot the guns. When 250 Confederate reinforcements from the Fourth Louisiana Battalion arrived and poured heavy fire at the Third New Hampshire, they were forced to withdraw.

By 9:00 a.m. the Union forces had suffered such heavy losses that they withdrew. Union casualties were 689 (107 dead). Their commander, Brigadier General Isaac Stevens, was said to have shed tears upon hearing of the loss of so many brave men. Confederate casualties were 207 with the loss of 52 men.

The Charleston Battalion bore the brunt of the attack with 49 officers wounded, killed or captured. Two prominent casualties were Charlestonians Captain Henry C. King and Lieutenant John Edwards, both of whom could have avoided the engagement had they not felt honor bound to serve their country. Lamar suffered a severe neck wound and was forced to pass command on to Lieutenant Colonel Peter C. Gaillard who was already severely wounded in the knee.[68]

Post battle reports rang with praise for the Charleston Battalion. Although it numbered 558 men on paper, due to "low country fever," detached duty to less arduous assignments, furlough and other considerations, only about 124 were actually present at the battle.

Colonel Johnson Hagood fought with such gallantry that he was promoted to Brigadier General. Gaillard succumbed to his wound and passed command to Major David Ramsey,[69] a well-educated and respected Charleston attorney.

Ramsay wrote the post-battle report that praised the defenders' bravery and mentioned in particular how Mr. Josiah Tennant of the Calhoun Guard "felled six of the enemy." He commended Captain William Ryan for handling a twenty-four-pounder gun. He honored three more for repeatedly bringing up ammunition through a heavy volume of enemy musketry; one was Sergeant Henry William Hendricks,[70] a peacetime deputy sheriff. Hendricks had also been dispatched to direct the movements of the Louisiana Battalion as they approached the battle. Hendricks succeeded "without receiving the slightest injury [and] resumed his place at the battery…It was a gallant and daring feat, eliciting the admiration of both men and officers."[71] Hendricks later told his family that bullets were flying around him as thick as hail as he dashed across the open field. When he passed a well, his first impulse was to jump in, but he continued on. This decision may have saved his life, for as he rushed by, he saw a shell explode in the well.

The *Charleston Mercury* reported, "The foe, it is true, displayed admirable courage. The famous Highland regiment, the Seventy-ninth New York occupied the prominent place in the picture, but their desperate onslaughts were of no avail against the stubborn resolve and lofty valor of our brave boys." The *Charleston Courier* editorialized that Secessionville was "another illustration of the deplorable consequences of this fratricidal war."

The plight of the Campbell brothers highlighted those consequences. During the battle, defending Lieutenant James Campbell mounted the parapet unarmed and rolled a log down into the advancing enemy. Meanwhile, his brother, Alexander Campbell, color bearer for the New York Seventy-ninth, planted the U.S. flag before the fort's parapet and kept it there until the New Yorkers were ordered to withdraw. It was only after the battle that the brothers realized that they had fought within yards of each other; afterward, they tried in vain to communicate during a flag of truce.

James and Alexander Campbell were sons of a Scots family that settled in New York City in the 1850s. James Campbell moved south to Charleston, where he worked as a drayman and a clerk. He joined the Union Light Infantry, sometimes called the Forty-second Highlanders, later consolidated into the Charleston Battalion.

Before the war, Alexander Campbell joined his brother in Charleston and worked as a stonemason on the new Custom House, then under construction. He enlisted in a local militia but returned to New York when the war started and joined the Seventy-ninth Highlander regiment.

After Secessionville, Alexander Campbell went on to Virginia and was wounded in the second battle of Manassas. He was promoted to second lieutenant but never fully recovered and resigned his commission in May 1863. He moved to Connecticut and established a business that manufactured "artistic monuments."

James Campbell continued in the defense of Charleston; he was taken prisoner during the second Union assault on Battery Wagner. He spent the remainder of the war in various Northern prison camps before he was released in June 1865. He returned to Charleston and bought land on the Ashepoo River. He was active in the St. Andrew's Society and the United Confederate Veterans. The brothers continued to correspond after the war; both died early in the twentieth century.[72]

After the fiasco at Secessionville, Union forces returned to Port Royal and began to build up a war machine to take Charleston. Three days after the attack, General Benham was arrested. The Judge Advocate General's Office recommended revocation of his commission, but it was rescinded because Hunter possessed an aggressiveness that most Union generals lacked in 1862. Benham went on to serve with Grant in Vicksburg and in the Virginia campaign.

General Beauregard returned to take command of the city's defenses; once the Federal stranglehold was broken, on August 19 martial law was revoked. Colonel Gaillard was detailed as provost marshal over Charleston. The Charleston Battalion was posted at various positions throughout the city during the winter.

Today historians theorize that had Secessionville fallen, the Union army would have flanked the harbor defenses and forced the Confederates to withdraw from Charleston. This would have established a base for operations in the interior and might have ended the war years earlier.

The victory at Secessionville purchased a year of relative peace in Charleston.

CHAPTER 12

The Union Strikes Back

1863–1864

THE IRONCLAD ATTACK

In September 1862, President Lincoln announced that he would emancipate all slaves in the Confederate states that did not return to the Union by January 1, 1863. As none complied, Lincoln used his war powers to issue a formal emancipation proclamation on January 1, 1863. The Proclamation made abolition a justification of the war, but it did not immediately affect Charleston.

After its humiliating defeat at Fredericksburg in December, the war-weary North was clamoring for a decisive victory. Assistant secretary of the navy, Gustavus Fox, in particular, was obsessed with capturing Charleston after his failure to relieve Fort Sumter two years earlier. He came up with the idea of destroying the shipping channels covered in the chapter entitled "Sinking of the Great Stone Fleet."

The Union navy had already assigned almost all of its armored vessels to the South Atlantic Blockading Squadron, and throughout the winter of 1862–63, Admiral Samuel F. DuPont prepared for an attack in Port Royal. The armada arrived off the coast of Charleston on April 7, almost exactly two years after the fall of Fort Sumter. The assault force consisted of seven single-turreted ironclad monitors and the 3,500-ton *New Ironsides* armed with sixteen Dahlgren guns and two Parrott rifles. Thirty wooden boats accompanied the ironclad fleet.

To support the maritime action, General David Benham had come up the coast and landed troops on Seabrook Island and Johns Island with the intent of conquering James Island. In response to the enemy buildup, the Confederate command deployed every available man to James Island and the harbor's entrance.

Charleston harbor was defended by sixty-three forts and batteries, as well as mines and submerged ropes designed to catch ships' propellers. The perimeter fortifications were so numerous they were said to resemble a porcupine with its quills turned out.

The ironclad attack was led by the monitor *Weehawken*, pushing a raft designed to detonate torpedoes. *Weehawken* was followed by three monitors, the mighty *New Ironsides* and finally four more monitors. (Percival Drayton was in command of the monitor *Passaic*, and Robert Smalls, the escaped river pilot, captained the experimental double-turreted *Keokuk*.)

A man of the old wooden navy, Admiral DuPont had little confidence in the new iron warships, and his worst fears were realized. The cumbersome ironclads were unable to navigate properly in the strong channel currents. Slowed down, they were caught in a heavy crossfire from Confederate defenses. The battle raged for over two hours. The Confederates fired 2,200 shots, and the Union ships retaliated with all they had to offer. All the while, curious spectators crowded onto the battery to witness the engagement.

The armored fleet was severely battered and withdrew at nightfall. DuPont fully intended to continue the assault the following day, but the attack never materialized. Five ironclads had been disabled, and the *Keokuk* had sustained ninety direct hits before it sank during the night.

DuPont's subordinates later persuaded him to withdraw, and towing the badly damaged vessels, the remaining ships slowly made their way back down the main channel. The smokestacks and gun turrets of the wrecked *Keokuk* near the harbor entrance remained as stark reminders of the fierce fight.

Some of *Keokuk*'s furniture, equipment and a signal code book washed up on Morris Island. Beauregard decided to salvage the wreck's two eleven-inch Dahlgren guns and hired the LaCoste brothers, civilian ship riggers. Over the next month, a volunteer crew worked under the cover of darkness, eighteen feet beneath the water's surface; they succeeded in removing their prizes right from under the noses of the blockading fleet. (One cannon was put at Fort Moultrie and one at Fort Sumter. The Fort Moultrie cannon now stands at the corner of East Battery and South Battery in White Point Garden in Charleston.)

The Ironclad Attack. *From* Harper's Weekly, *May 2, 1863.*

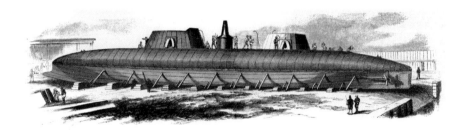

The *Keokuk* was commissioned March 1863 and sank off Morris Island on April 8, 1863. *From* Harper's Weekly, *April 25, 1863.*

General Hunter had not been ordered to attack and withdrew from Johns Island. He secretly fortified Folly and Coles Islands for a land assault that was still on the drawing board.

The abortive boat attack caused DuPont to lose favor with the Navy Department. At his own request, he was relieved of command in July 1863. After Admiral DuPont's reluctant resignation, command of the South Atlantic Blockading Squadron passed to Rear Admiral John Dahlgren, a personal friend of President Lincoln. Dahlgren had headed the Union navy's Ordnance Department where he had designed several different kinds of guns, including one which bears his name.

Battery Wagner

If the Union hoped to destroy Fort Sumter, it was obvious to Washington strategists that after the ironclad debacle, a combined naval and army operation would be required. Needing more aggressive leadership, Brigadier General Quincy A. Gillmore was called from Kentucky to replace General Hunter. Gillmore had become a national hero after reducing Fort Pulaski in Savannah. He had graduated top of his class at West Point and was considered the foremost authority on rifled artillery and engineering operations.

The agreed-upon strategy was to silence the guns at Battery Wagner (called Fort Wagner by the North) and Battery Gregg on Morris Island, a sandbar that protected part of the harbor and the main ship channel. From there, Gillmore was to destroy Fort Sumter's offensive capabilities and gain control of Charleston harbor. Secretary Wells promised that if those objectives were accomplished, the ironclads could finish what remained to be done to capture the city.

Gillmore reached Hilton Head on June 12, 1863, and quickly proceeded to Folly Island to reconnoiter Morris Island across the inlet.

Morris Island was located on the west side of Charleston's outer harbor, and at the time of the war, it was described as stretching three miles from north to south. A ridge of white sand hills ran parallel with the beach, just out of reach of the tidal line on the east, while the west sloped into marshes two miles wide, intersected by a labyrinth of watercourses that separated it from James Island. It was an island of fine white sand where, at a few points, the tide broke entirely across it. (Today, due to accretion, Morris Island is almost completely submerged.)

Union troops secretly began building batteries on Folly Island behind a thicket only a few hundred yards from Confederate defenses across the inlet. Work crews were landed at night, and before morning, they hid behind the dense foliage; the troop transports were sent away before dawn. Hidden from view by the brushwood, the troops finished the batteries in twenty days. Each battery was fortified with forty-eight mounted guns and mortars, bomb-proofs, ammunition, magazines, etc. The clandestine construction was so successful that the Confederates did not suspect the Union presence until they cut away the bushes concealing the batteries shortly before they opened fire on the morning of July 10.

Gillmore hoped to overpower the Confederates by sheer manpower and underestimated the Confederate defenses. The first phase of the operation went well. Covered by batteries on Folly Island and the naval guns offshore,

General Quincy A. Gillmore in front of his tent on Morris Island. *Library of Congress.*

Union troops landed at Lighthouse Point on the southern end of the island. General George Crockett Strong was so anxious to get ashore that he stepped into seven feet of water and lost his boots; he recovered quickly and, barefoot, mounted a captured Confederate horse without a saddle and galloped off in pursuit of the enemy.

In spite of brave resistance, the Confederates were quickly overwhelmed by the superior forces. In little more than four hours, two thousand invaders routed Confederate defenses and took two-thirds of Morris Island with a loss of only twelve men.

It was an intensely hot and humid July day, and according to a Union general who participated in the action, the troops were nearly prostrate. Resting on his laurels, Gillmore decided to let his men recover before attacking Battery Wagner. This turned out to be a huge mistake, for the respite gave the Confederate defenders time to prepare for the battle during the night.

The following day, Gillmore launched a direct assault on Battery Wagner, then under the command of Brigadier General William B. Taliaferro, a seasoned veteran of Stonewall Jackson's campaigns. The fort was well sited with walls of sand and earth supported by palmetto logs and sandbags. It had fourteen cannons and a bombproof shelter capable of shielding one

Ruins of Charleston Lighthouse, Morris Island (vicinity), South Carolina. *Library of Congress.*

thousand men. The fort was protected by a five-foot-deep water-filled trench, land mines and sharpened palmetto stakes. The attack was repulsed and cost 330 Union lives; only 12 Confederates were killed in the action.

After the unsuccessful attack, Gillmore decided to pulverize Battery Wagner before launching another assault. Coordinating with the navy offshore, on the morning of July 18, the guns of the blockading fleet joined the land forces in a continuous barrage that lasted from dawn to dusk. The intense bombardment was later described as causing the whole island to smoke like a furnace and tremble like an earthquake. During the shelling, most of the Confederate defenders crowded into the fort's bombproof shelter.

The three hundred men in Colonel Gaillard's Charleston Battalion requested the dangerous task of manning the ramparts. They had no protection except the parapet. Remarkably, Gaillard was able to boast later that his men were not demoralized by the experience. This was due primarily to the bravery of their officers. Gaillard moved from position to position to steady his men; twice he was half-buried in sand when shells exploded nearby.

The unflappable Major David Ramsay sat in a chair in the middle of the parade ground calmly reading a newspaper. Whenever Ramsay rose to help a wounded man, he deliberately folded his paper, providing a cool and imperturbable example that helped keep up the spirits of the exposed

Unidentified artillery unit, Morris Island, South Carolina. *Library of Congress.*

Battery "B" of the last U.S. artillery (Henry's battery), active during siege operations against Fort Wagner and Battery Gregg, Morris Island, South Carolina. *Library of Congress.*

citizen soldiers. When the flag was blown off the flagstaff, Major Ramsey and several others rushed up to the parapet and reattached it in spite of intense enemy fire.

At twilight, gunfire rose to a crescendo as the Union army assembled on the beach and prepared to launch its frontal assault. Dusk was chosen because the light was sufficient for the troops to advance but dim enough to prevent accurate fire by the enemy.

The charge was led by Colonel Robert Gould Shaw of the Fifty-fourth Massachusetts Volunteers, a regiment of black soldiers commanded by white officers. This heroic charge has since been immortalized in the 1989 movie *Glory*.

When Shaw was killed in action, Captain Louis F. Emilio of New York City became their acting commander. Emilio later wrote that before the attack, Shaw's "bearing was composed and graceful, his cheek had somewhat paled, and the slight twitching of the corners of his mouth plainly showed that the whole cost was counted." (Shaw's youthful sacrifice was lionized in the North. In addition to contemporary praises, forty poems were written in his honor, and long after his death, a handsome monument by Augustus Saint-Gaudens was erected on Boston Common on Memorial Day 1897.)

After fierce fighting on both sides, the Union soldiers withdrew when it became evident that they could not take the fort. Though wounded in four places, Sergeant William Carney was able to bring away the national flag and later became the first African American soldier awarded the Congressional Medal of Honor.

During the engagement, defending Major Ramsay was accidentally shot in the back by friendly fire. He was taken home and died on Broad Street on August 4. He was mourned as "one of the 'bright, peculiar stars' of South Carolina…this scholar, statesman, soldier, gentleman…unsurpassed in intellect…at heart a lover of the Union he fought to destroy, but a martyr to the State to which he deemed his allegiance was due." His funeral took place at Central Presbyterian (Circular) churchyard on Meeting Street, where he was buried next to his illustrious grandfather, Dr. David Ramsay.[73]

Captain Willaim H. Ryan was of Irish descent. He captured prisoners at Secessionville in 1862 and fought at the Battle of Sol Legare Island on July 3, 1863, before he was killed at Battery Wagner gallantly leading an attack on enemy troops entrenched on the top of the bombproof shelter. The *Mercury* commented, "Few men have fallen more universally lamented in our community…Of a handsome mein, unobtrusive and kind manner, his acquaintance was large and his friends all who knew him."

The morning after the attack revealed appalling carnage. Of the 5,000 Union troops committed to action, 1,515 mangled bodies lay strewn about the battleground. In the ditch before the battery, the dead were stacked four deep in some places. Confederate losses were 226 killed, wounded or missing.

The next day, Union soldiers requested a cease-fire to bury their dead, but the Confederates suspected that it was a ploy to spy on the fort and denied the request. Due to the sweltering July heat, General Hagood ordered burial as quickly as possible.

Storming Fort Wagner, by Kurz and Allison. *Library of Congress.*

Colonel Shaw's corpse was treated shamefully by some of the Confederate soldiers. His body was stripped of its uniform and placed in a common trench beneath his black soldiers. A Confederate officer later commented, "This desecration of the dead we endeavored to provide against; but at that time…our men were so frenzied that it was next to impossible to guard against it," explaining that Shaw's desecration was "by the more desperate and lower class of our troops."[74] When news of this reached the North, some were so scandalized that they tried to have Shaw's body exhumed and buried with full military honors. Only the intervention by Shaw's father put an end to the Northern outcry.

Twenty-four black troops of the Massachusetts Fifty-fourth were taken prisoner. Unlike their white compatriots, they were not exchanged for Confederate prisoners and were imprisoned in the old Charleston jail awaiting justice meted out under an 1863 Confederate law. In South Carolina, this meant that they were regarded as insurrection slaves. They were ordered to stand trial, and their fate seemed certain, for a gallows had already been erected in the jail's courtyard.

President Lincoln had warned that a Confederate prisoner would be put to death every time a Union soldier was executed. Fearing reprisals on

Union camp on Morris Island. *Courtesy Library of Congress.*

Confederate prisoners of war, the military probably pressured the court not to execute, for it unexpectedly admitted that they had no jurisdiction in the case. Giving blacks equal status with the white population was such an explosive decision that even the *Mercury* dared not publish. Authorities never attempted to put the black soldiers on trial again.

Although the assault at Battery Wagner had little significance militarily, it had a huge impact on the North, for it proved that African American troops could, and would, fight for their country. General Gillmore ordered that his forces be integrated. Black soldiers were no longer assigned only menial tasks, such as latrine duty and kitchen duties, but instead were to carry arms into battle. (In 1864, President Lincoln publicly stated that the Union cause could not prevail without the contribution of one hundred thousand black soldiers then in uniform.)

An interesting footnote to the battle is that the Union leaders did not realize that the enemy had broken their signal code. Major K. Pliny Bryan, a Confederate officer, had been placed among the Union signal men captured on John's Island, and he had succeeded in getting them to reveal the code key. The most difficult part of interpreting signals was to determine whether the distant signal operator had his face or back to the person reading the signal.

After the arduous duty of watching the parapet of Fort Sumter without relief for four consecutive days and nights, T. Pinckney Lowndes had the distinction of first intercepting the Union signal, a wig-wag message from the new ironclad to Morris Island. In it, Admiral Dahlgren informed General Gillmore about massing of the fleet's small boats in the Lighthouse Inlet in order to convey troops to Morris Island.

Another announcement of the Federal intention to assault Battery Wagner was conveyed in a signal intercepted by signalman Millard, a sergeant in Lowndes' corps, on July 16. "Keep your infantry under arms; the men must remain in line. The island is filled with stragglers." Another message read, "An assault is ordered at dusk. Husband your ammunition, so as to deliver a rapid fire the last half hour." [75]

The Swamp Angel

Once Gillmore was finally convinced that Battery Wagner was too strong to be taken by direct assault, he decided to destroy Fort Sumter by shooting *over* Battery Wagner. Although this tactic was contrary to conventional military engineering of the day, he proceeded to erect eight heavily armed batteries.

While bombarding Fort Sumter, some land-based shots were fired in the direction of Charleston. They nearly reached the city, and Colonel Edward Serrell of the New York Volunteer Engineers suggested that they could bombard Charleston directly if a gun were mounted farther to the west.

Less than a week after taking the southern part of Morris Island, Gillmore sent engineers to scout for a suitable location for a gun. They spent days conducting a series of experiments to locate soil capable of supporting a battery. A spot was chosen where a pole could be run down sixteen feet before hitting bottom. It was located in marsh about a mile from Morris Island on the edge of a creek that served as a wet ditch.

Gilmore immediately approved the plan. Construction of the battery was assigned to a lieutenant of engineers who flatly stated that the work was impossible. Colonel Serrell ordered him to requisition the necessary materials. The next day a request was made for one hundred men eighteen feet tall to wade through mud sixteen feet deep; the lieutenant also called upon the department's surgeon to inquire if he could splice three six-foot men together if they were furnished. His commanding officer was not amused, and the pleasantry cost the lieutenant his arrest.

On August 2, 1863, fatigue parties from the Seventh New Hampshire began erecting a 1,700-yard, 4-foot-wide plank causeway across the marsh to the designated spot. Eight days later, they began work on the battery. First, a rectangular frame of sheet piling was driven into the marsh by a hand-lever-operated driver. Then a three-sided grillage of logs was bolted onto the pilings, leaving a rectangular aperture for the gun platform.

The marsh battery was an engineering marvel. The gun deck was not connected to the platform but floated on the marsh in equilibrium. The base was constructed with packed-down marsh grass, canvas and sand that was topped with a plank platform. The effort required thousands of feet of board and planking, pine timbers, hundreds of feet of three-inch rope and 1,200 pounds of spikes and nails.

More than eight hundred tons of sandbags were transported to the battery at a cost of $5,000. Lugging heavy weights on the slippery planks sometimes caused the men to fall into the marsh, and they were occasionally shot at by soldiers guarding James Island. The men did not understand the purpose of the hard labor and disparagingly called the disagreeable project the "Marsh Croker," "Mud Lark" and "Serrell's Folly."

The giant gun arrived two weeks later. First the 8,000-pound carriage was hauled to the edge of the marsh and put on a raft and ferried out to the battery. It was followed by the huge 16,300-pound, eight-inch rifled Parrott, which had been placed on a customized boat that had only five inches of freeboard after the gun was positioned. The trip was tedious, for water had to be constantly pumped out of the boat. Before morning, however, the giant gun was loaded onto the platform; it was mounted four days later.

The marsh battery was manned by a detachment from the Eleventh Maine Infantry, which had been brought up from Fernandina, Florida. Once readied for action, the gun's sights were set on St. Michael's steeple.[76] The name Swamp Angel is said to have been suggested by Sergeant Feller of the New York Volunteer Engineers.

After most of Morris Island had been overrun, General Beauregard asked local planters to supply slaves to shore up the defenses on James Island. Most refused, claiming that they had already provided as much labor as required by the military. The *Mercury* took them to task, stating that this was a grave mistake, and for the next few days, the paper published appeals for help with sandbags.

On August 21, Gillmore was informed that the battery had been completed. He wrote General Beauregard a letter threatening to shell the city if the Confederates failed to evacuate Morris Island and Fort Sumter. Beauregard was away inspecting batteries in the countryside and could not be reached. His staff tried to stall the ultimatum by returning the dispatch with a terse note asking for verification since it had not been properly signed.

Vendue Range. Building on left is where the first shell struck the city. *Library of Congress.*

Gillmore saw through the ruse. Upon the orders of President Lincoln, at 1:30 a.m. on August 29, the Swamp Angel commenced firing incendiary projectiles called "Greek Fire" into the streets of Charleston. No official warning had been given, and the first explosion caused pandemonium as bells, whistles and alarms echoed through the city's streets and awakened thousands of innocent women and children. Residents made preparations to evacuate, and large trains left after daylight, loaded with families not knowing where they were going but willing to go anywhere to escape.

The next morning, a properly signed note from Gillmore was received at Beauregard's headquarters. The enraged general responded, "Among

Bursting of a shell in Charleston, South Carolina. (*Harper's Weekly.*) *Library of Congress.*

nations not barbarous the use of war prescribes that when a city is about to be attacked, timely notice shall be given by the attacking command, in order that noncombatants may have an opportunity for withdrawing beyond its limits….you now resort to the novel measure of turning your guns against the old men, the women and children, and the hospitals of a sleeping city, an act of inexcusable barbarity."

Gillmore gave Beauregard one day to clear the city of noncombatants. Many of the city's residents had already left town and those who remained in the lower part of the city moved out of range of the siege guns. Shelling resumed on the next evening, and fortunately for Charleston, the Parrott gun exploded on the thirty-sixth shot and blew the barrel on top of the parapet.

It didn't take William Gilmore Simms long to pen a poem decrying the "sacrilegious aim" at St. Michael's Church. Up North the public was delighted. Even Herman Melville waged in with:

The Union Strikes Back: 1864-1864

"'The Grand Skedaddle' of the inhabitants from Charleston, South Carolina, when threatened by an attack from the Union troops, from a sketch by Lieutenant G.P. Kirby, Forty-seventh New York Volunteers, when a prisoner in Charleston." (*Frank Leslie's Illustrated* January 17, 1863.) *Courtesy Charleston Museum, Charleston, South Carolina.*

The Swamp Angel platform after the explosion with the eight-inch Parrott lying on top of the platform. *Library of Congress.*

There is a coal-black Angel
With a thick Afric-lip,
And he dwells (like the haunted and Harried)
In a swamp where the green frongs dip…

The Swamp Angel was the first known artillery piece to use a compass reading, and its shells reached farther than any previous projectiles. General Gillmore enjoys the notoriety of being one of the first generals to bombard a civilian center for a military objective. With its military career over, the Swamp Angel was slated to be sold as scrap iron when citizens of Trenton, New Jersey, bought the historic gun and turned it into a Civil War monument.

Confederates Evacuate Morris Island

Day by day, the Yankees dug trenches that zig-zagged closer to Fort Wagner while the ironclads shelled Confederate defenses with impunity. The siege became a virtual laboratory for new military technology. Federal gunners, for example, experimented with so-called Requa batteries, forerunners of the machine gun, which consisted of twenty-five rifles arranged horizontally, which could fire up to 175 shots per minute. At night, engineers aimed huge calcium lights at the fort to prevent the Confederates from rebuilding the day's damage—the first use of search lights in military history.

On August 17, the troops were within range to fire on Fort Sumter. A thousand shells were fired the first day. By August 23, Sumter's masonry had been turned to rubble. In all, 6,250 projectiles were fired at the beleaguered fort; the scream of shot and shell was fearful, and every hit was followed by a cloud of brick and dust. The ironclads took part in the last day of the bombardment, although they withdrew before finishing off the fort.

Morris Island was a hellhole for the men on both sides. Brigadier General W.W. Davis, who served under Gillmore, described the rigors of the besieging troops:

Those who have not engaged in such operations can have only a faint idea
of the labor and fatigue attending the construction of the batteries and
mounting the guns. The three-hundred-pounder gave great trouble before it
was got into position. It was transported more than a mile from the dock,

Federal mortars on Morris Island aimed at Fort Sumter. *Library of Congress.*

through deep sands, and across semi-marsh overflowed by the tide. It broke down three slingcarts. It was about a week on the way, and in the daytime it was covered with brush and weeds to conceal it from the enemy. Not only were the batteries mostly built, but all the guns were mounted, at night. Most of the work was done under fire.[77]

The Union's trenching efforts near Battery Wagner began to expose corpses buried after the two assaults. In the harsh conditions, many of the

Union soldiers became ill or died, causing the medical inspector to report that unless Battery Wagner fell quickly, the troops could be in no condition to execute the siege and further opined that a third assault would be more economical of life than a continuance of the present operations.

The continuous bombardment took its toll on the Confederates. Eventually, nearly every one of the fort's fixed guns was blown from its position. According to Colonel Charles C. Jones, the interior of Battery Wagner "was little else than a charnel house. Its polluted atmosphere almost refused to support life, and its galleries were filled with the groans of the wounded and dying. Temperatures soared over 100 degrees. Sand insinuated itself into men's eyes and noses, their clothes, their food, and their equipment. Mosquitoes swarmed everywhere. Fevers, scurvy, and dysentery took growing toll."[78]

On August 23, Colonel Gaillard was injured when a shell shattered his left hand and wrist. His hand was amputated, and he was relieved of his command and sent back to Charleston.

Beauregard changed Fort Sumter's garrison from artillery to infantry. In anticipation of the evacuation of Morris Island, he ordered removal of all but the three guns facing the main ship channel. On the night of September 4, Fort Sumter officially became an infantry post manned by the Charleston Battalion.

On September 5, the combined guns of General Gillmore and Admiral Dahlgren bombarded Battery Wagner for forty hours without cessation. The air was filled with shells bursting in and over the fort, forcing the defenders to seek shelter beneath the bomb-proof. At night the spectacle was so grand that observers later commented that the heavens seemed alive with fiery projectiles. The Confederates lost 125 men in spite of the bomb-proof protection.

When the Union captured Wagner's rifle pits, Colonel Lawrence M. Keitt informed Beauregard that he had only four hundred men capable of defending the fort. Bowing to the inevitable, during the night of September 6–7, the Confederates fled to Charleston, justifiably proud of the fact that for fifty-eight days, a garrison of less than one thousand men had held off a force of eleven thousand supported by superior armaments firing from both land and sea. Upon his safe arrival in Charleston, one defender was heard to say that he wasn't "afeared of hell no more—it can't touch Wagner."

The next day, eager Union troops were surprised to find that the fort had been deserted and only a few laggards remained to be taken prisoner.

FORT SUMTER HOLDS FAST

On September 7, Admiral Dahlgren demanded Fort Sumter's surrender. Beauregard replied that he could have the fort if he could take it. Dahlgren decided to capture the irksome symbol of rebellion the following night. General Gillmore had planned a similar operation that same evening. Wanting to claim credit for the navy, Admiral Dahlgren refused to put his men under the army command. Thus, two independent forces set off to capture Fort Sumter. Low tide detained the army boats off Morris Island while Dahlgren proceeded according to plan.

Dahlgren had a penchant for intelligence gathering and had personally questioned escaped Union prisoners and Confederate deserters brought aboard his flagship. He did not realize that the signal flag communications between the fleet and the army had been intercepted by a Confederate signalman on deck of the ironclad *Chicora*.

Wanting to personally witness the historic event, Dahlgren was rowed to an observation point near the fort. With the prize almost within his grasp, he watched Commodore Thomas H. Stevens approach the fort with a flotilla of thirty boats carrying more than eight hundred marines and sailors.

Forewarned, the Confederates held their fire until the boats were nearly ashore, then they blasted the exposed Yankees with everything from hand grenades to brickbats; the guns of CSS *Chicora* and the Confederate island batteries joined in. Surprised at the strong resistance, Dahlgren withdrew, and the landing party surrendered. The assault cost the Union 127 killed, wounded or taken captive. The Confederates did not suffer any casualties. Luckily for General Gillmore, by the time his boats could proceed, the naval assault had already been defeated.[79]

A second bombardment of Fort Sumter commenced on October 26 and lasted unabated until December 6. Members of the Charleston Battalion continued to defend Fort Sumter in spite of continuous bombardment and living underground like moles. On November 28, Private James Tupper Jr. walked the whole length of the gorge wall on the parapet to raise the flag when it was shot down. Finding the staff too short, he procured an additional spar and with the assistance of some comrades, succeeded in splicing and planting the staff under such heavy fire that twice the flag was shot from their hands.[80]

In December, the telegraph connection between Charleston and Fort Sumter failed after the receiver was smashed by shellfire. Although exposed to enemy shelling, Lieutenant Colonel William Richard Cathcart, a telegraph

Signalmen of Rear Admiral John A. Dahlgren's flagship. *Library of Congress.*

operator, managed to keep communications open by receiving the dots and dashes on his tongue. Then the wire suddenly went dead. Only three hundred yards from the enemy, Cathcart and George W. Kates, superintendent of Confederate telegraph lines and signal corps, tried to locate the break during three bitterly cold December nights. Kates went out in a rowboat while Cathcart floated on a mattress endeavoring to locate the break, which they assumed was underwater. Cathcart paid for his brave deed by suffering from severe arthritis ever after. On December 18, Beauregard commended

Cathcart for behaving "with remarkable courage and energy. In no branch of the military service is coolness and determination more necessary than in the telegraph and signal corps, for on their bravery and attention to duty in trying moments often depend the results of the most important military affairs. The conduct of Mr. Cathcart is commended to the emulation of the members of the telegraph service throughout the department."[81]

Gillmore was promoted to Major General after conquering Morris Island. Once his forces consolidated their position, they turned their sights on Charleston and bombarded the city mercilessly. Although twenty-two thousand shells made their way to the city, miraculously, only sixty-four civilians were killed.

When Beauregard advised Gillmore that he had Union prisoners as well as women and children within the reach of his guns, firing at that square of the city was stopped after two days. In August 1864, in retaliation

180 Broad Street, the O'Connor House, in which eighty-three Union officers were confined under fire after the Swamp Angel and other shells were fired into Charleston. Sketched by one of the officers. (*Harper's Weekly*, August 27, 1864.) *Courtesy Charleston Museum, Charleston, South Carolina.*

for placing Union troops within range of the bombardment, six hundred Confederate officers were transferred from Fort Delaware to a Union stockade on Morris Island, where they remained exposed to fire from Confederate guns for two months.

The siege of Charleston has been described as the longest campaign of the Civil War. In spite of a vast expenditure of lives and munitions, the North had still not taken the city. In May 1864, General Gillmore asked to be reassigned. He was replaced by Major General John G. Foster who, with a force of fifteen thousand men, tried to conquer Charleston, then defended by five thousand Confederates. Union forces made several attempts to conquer Fort Johnson, but the Confederates stubbornly resisted their efforts throughout the remainder of 1864.

CHAPTER 13

Gaillard's Regiment Goes North

1864–1865

Prior to the war, Johnson Hagood had been a brigadier general in the state militia. He became a colonel of the First South Carolina Volunteers and had assisted in the battle of Fort Sumter in 1861. He served at Manassas and returned to James Island in June 1862. He was promoted to brigadier general after the battle of Secessionville and relieved Taliaferro at Battery Wagner on July 19, 1863. He commanded several tours on James Island before General Beauregard created a new brigade for his command in September 1863.

The troops were the best Beauregard had to offer in the entire Department of South Carolina, Georgia and eastern Florida. Among them was the intrepid Charleston Battalion, which had distinguished itself in every major assault upon the Confederate defenses of Charleston. Beauregard brought the Charleston Battalion up to a full regiment with the addition of three sharpshooter units, much to the consternation of both the outsiders from other parts of South Carolina and the men in the Charleston Battalion. The new regiment was officially named the Twenty-seventh South Carolina Infantry Regiment. Peter Gaillard was promoted to full colonel and given command with the assumption that he would fully recover from the amputation of his left hand. Although men from all over the state had been added, the Twenty-seventh retained its Charleston identity and soon came to be known simply as "Gaillard's Regiment."[82]

Throughout the fall and into the winter of 1863–64, the Twenty-seventh stood watch over Charleston and trained repeatedly for the action yet to come. This is the story of one man who lived to tell the tale.

THE WAR DIARY

Former deputy sheriff Henry William Hendricks volunteered to join when the first call to arms was made and served during all the Union assaults around Charleston. When Gaillard's regiment was ordered north on April 28, 1864, he began recording his experiences in a diary.

In the spring of 1864, Ulysses S. Grant began his final assault on Virginia, coming at the Confederate government in Richmond by simultaneously advancing south against the Army of Northern Virginia and by marching west with a second army along the James River from Hampton Roads with a second army under General Benjamin (Beast) Butler; a third army destroyed Lee's food supply with a "scorched earth" march through the Shenandoah Valley.

With Charleston at a stalemate, General Beauregard was summoned north to defend against Butler's advances along the James River. Coincidentally, General Gillmore had joined General Butler's command, bringing with him twenty thousand seasoned veterans, leaving only enough men in South Carolina to continue shelling Charleston and to keep the sea islands they had already captured.

It took Gaillard's brigade of 526 men nine days of weary rail travel to reach Petersburg, Virginia. Upon arrival, they were almost immediately engaged in skirmishes, and within a week, they had participated defending the massive Confederate fortification at Drury's Bluff. They pursued the enemy, fighting at Bermuda Hundred in mid-May and at Cold Harbor on May 31.

In his diary, Hendricks described the dead Yankees lying for three days between the two camps at Bermuda Hundred, catching "two grey backs" on his clothes, having a "fine wash," writing his wife and eating a good steak when a deer was shot. Interestingly, the pickets in both camps wanted to trade tobacco for sugar and coffee, but the Southerners were not allowed to trade or communicate with the enemy.

Hendricks gave a daily account of the Battle of Cold Harbor, considered one of the bloodiest battles of the war. The two armies faced each other for nine grueling days of trench warfare. The trenches were hot, dusty

"BELLE PLAIN, Virginia, the recent base of supplies for General Grant's army, is simply a rude landing on Potomac Creek, constructed for the present emergency, right at the foot of a range of wooded hills, along which sharp, precipitous roads wind away towards Fredericksburg. There are no houses of any sort within a mile of the landing, and the appearance of the surrounding country is desolate in the extreme. The offing… was constantly crowded with transports and naval vessels, receiving and unloading stores and troops; and the scene from the heights on a clear day was almost as full of life and animation as New York Harbor." (*Harpers Weekly*, June 11, 1864.) *Image courtesy Library of Congress.*

and miserable. By the third day, Hendricks wrote that a North Carolina Confederate major raised a white flag to surrender. He was shot at by his own colonel, and when that shot missed, the colonel ordered his men to shoot him down. The fighting was fierce, with many dead lying between the two opposing forces.

Grant at Cold Harbor. *Library of Congress.*

Torn railroad lines. *Library of Congress.*

Although Lee offered Grant a flag of truce to bury his dead, Grant refused because he did not want to signal that he had lost the battle. As a result, wounded Union soldiers lay among the dead waving their hands for help until they too, became bloated corpses. (Hendricks called General Grant an "old brute.") It is estimated that the Union lost somewhere between 7,000 and 13,000 men compared to Lee's 1,000 to 1,500.

The Twenty-seventh was redeployed to Petersburg. When Captain Brown was killed in the trenches, Hendricks was promoted to captain and retained that position until the end of the war. At one time, he was the only officer in his company who had not been killed or taken prisoner.

Hendricks was hospitalized with a fever and was sent by train to a Raleigh hospital, "a mean place with straw beds full of bed bugs." He was later transferred to Columbia, which he described as "one of the last places God has allowed to be called a hospital." He was released at the end of June and sent to Weldon by train.

With the rails torn up, the men were forced to march the last twenty-five miles to Petersburg. The road was dusty, and they had nothing to eat, for the local farmers were starving. Back in the trenches on July 9, the men were given a small piece of bacon, three spoons of corn bread and a spoonful of rice for the day. The meager food supply caused rations to be stolen. Heavy rains made the trenches "as near a hog pen as it is possible for them to be. I sleep on logs tonight to keep myself off the ground."

Being constantly shelled by the enemy and the harsh conditions affected Hendricks's health, and within two weeks, he was back in the infirmary where he ate "the best meals in the past six months."

Returning to the front, he described always feeling sick, correspondence with his family and the tedium of trench warfare: fatigue duty, intense heat, poor rations, intermittent fighting. On one occasion when going to the front after a rainstorm, the men forded rushing water that came up to their armpits; another time General Hagood ordered a drain dug to draw water from flooded trenches.

In early August, the troops were deployed to Weldon to recapture a portion of the railroad that linked Petersburg and Richmond with Wilmington and Charleston. On August 4, Hendricks was captured and was taken to "Yankeeland." Although he didn't know it at the time, this probably saved his life, for Hagood's charge occurred twenty days later.

Before approaching Weldon, General Hagood had been assured that no field works had been established. However, when his men came out of the woods, they encountered rifle pits and heavily manned earthworks. The discovery was made too late, for the "rebel yell" had already rung out loud and clear as determined men cleared the heavily armed rifle pits. Without anticipated reinforcements, the Confederates were trapped in a heavy crossfire. Once the standard bearers had all been killed, Union Captain Daly of General Butler's staff rode out and took possession of the brigade's colors. Escape seemed hopeless, and he urged the Confederates to surrender. General Hagood stepped boldly forward and demanded the colors back and offered Daly safe passage back to his lines. When he refused, Hagood shot him, and as Daly fell from his horse, the general leaped into the empty saddle, tossing the colors to Dwight Stoney.

The brigade rallied and fought its way back through withering firepower. The Federal line to the rear collapsed as they charged through it. When

Washington, D.C. The Old Capitol Prison, First and A Streets NE. *Library of Congress.*

Hagood's horse was killed, he led his men on foot back across half a mile of open field while deadly enemy fire pursued them all the way to the cover of the swamp. Of the 681 men who made the charge, 292 returned to the Confederate lines.

While Hagood was preparing for Weldon, Hendricks and other prisoners were taken to Fort McHenry near Baltimore. From there, they were transported to the Old Capitol Prison in Washington, where they were not allowed to look out of the windows. A sentinel was posted below with orders to shoot them if they were caught. (Hendricks mentions that Confederate spy Belle Boyd was also in the prison at that time.)

The men were soon transferred to a filthy prison in Philadelphia that was full of lice and bedbugs. Eight days after their capture, the prisoners found themselves in notorious Fort Delaware on Pea Patch Island. It was a forbidding place that had been enlarged just before the war. The exterior walls were made of solid granite blocks, which were surrounded by a moat and drawbridge. The prisoners were housed in overcrowded brick barracks.

About 2,700 of the 12,500 prisoners died during incarceration; many were buried at Finn's Point, New Jersey, just across the Delaware River.

Fort Delaware was a muddy, vermin-infested place manned with the guards who were "very low fellows for soldiers." On one occasion, the guards made three officers walk up and down the yard on the double quick for two hours at the point of bayonets. The only food provided was slops, stale bread, half-done beans and water soup. Those without money from home were literally starving to death.

To survive, prisoners resorted to catching and frying rats and fishing for catfish in the open "sinks" where the men relieved themselves. Many were so sick that they used quart bottles for chamber pots, as the walk to the sinks was too exhausting. They passed the time playing cards, pitching horseshoes, shooting marbles, catching catfish and killing rats. Conditions were so deplorable that someone exclaimed that "there was no Hell," echoing the very words of Andersonville prisoners who were crowded into a filthy Georgia stockade where almost a quarter of the prisoners died from malnutrition, dysentery and exposure.

On September 16, the walls at Fort Delaware were whitewashed to help rid the barracks of lice. Three weeks later, the two sides began exchanging prisoners. Hendricks knew that the sick prisoners would be exchanged first. Before the surgeons examined him, he licked the newly-painted wall and thoroughly coated his tongue with whitewash. The surgeon who examined him exclaimed, "He'll die in three weeks!" and ordered him released. Hendricks was paroled thirty-five days after his arrival.

He passed his thirty-eighth birthday at Atkins Landing en route to Charleston. Their transport had a band on board, and the men could hardly keep from crying at the sight of the Confederate flag. Hendricks was furloughed for two months. The diary is silent during his leave, but family records show that his fifth child was born on December 14, just five days before he was ordered to rejoin his brigade.

December 19, 1864, found Hendricks headed to Wilmington, North Carolina. The cold weather and trees encrusted with ice matched his dour mood. On Christmas Day, he was on a steamer headed down the Cape Fear River in a rain that drenched to the skin. Hendricks made several entries about renegade Confederates who shamefully destroyed civilian household property and wantonly killed civilian livestock, leaving the carcasses rotting in open fields. The cold rain continued intermittently as the men made a hard fifteen-mile march through the "meanest country" yet. By the time they reached their destination, the men were caked with mud and some got sick again.

Gaillard's Regiment Goes North: 1864-1865

After a brief sojourn in the encampment near Wilmington, the regiment was ordered to the heavily fortified Cape Fear River. Wilmington was the Confederacy's last open port, and both sides knew that if the Cape Fear defenses fell, the Southern cause was doomed.

On January 12, 1865, an armada of fifty-six ships began bombarding Fort Fisher in the largest amphibious operation until World War II. The heavily fortified fort was built mostly of soil, making its structure extremely efficient at absorbing attacks from heavy artillery.

Eight thousand Union soldiers landed on January 15 and entered the massive fortification. The Confederates found themselves battling behind their own walls and were forced to retreat. They blew up forts on the north side of the river before crossing to defend Fort Anderson, another pivotal fortification protecting Wilmington.

By January 15, Hendricks had a miserable chest cold that was compounded by the demoralizing battle losses and news of the evacuation of Charleston. The men were almost starving but faced almost certain death or capture if they left their protected positions. On February 20, Hendricks was captured again; he was taken to Fort Anderson, where it was galling to hear his captors "crow" about the fall of Charleston and the news that the war would probably end in a couple of days.

On February 23, Hendricks was put aboard a prisoner transport named *Tonawanda*. The men became seasick as the ship tossed in an overnight storm. It was a difficult trip. Over five hundred men were crowded in a hold that reeked of vomit and the stench of human waste. Only two men were allowed on deck at a time. As a result, the rest of the men were forced to "do their business" in two barrels. During a storm, these barrels overturned and dumped their contents onto the men who were lying nearby. Henricks commented that the hold reminded him of the slave trade and its attendant suffering. It was four days before the wretched ship reached Fortress Munro and was cleaned up by the prisoners.

The Confederate captives were taken to the Old Capitol prison in Washington just before Lincoln's inaugural celebration. They were treated as badly as before, this time for revenge for the way the Yankees prisoners were treated in Andersonville. Hendricks continued to complain about the skimpy rations and the bleakness of the cause. On the third of March, he witnessed the execution of a Yankee sergeant who had raped and murdered an eight-year-old girl. He was shot in the prison yard, and Hendricks commented that in spite of his crimes, the soldier "died like a man." Diary entries stop on March 9, 1865.

Hagood's Brigade served under General Joseph E. Johnson in North Carolina at the end of the war and surrendered at Durham Station in April 1865. Due to wartime attrition, only seven men remained when the Charleston Brigade was officially disbanded on May 3, 1865, at the Lancaster Courthouse in South Carolina.[83]

Colonel Peter Charles Gailliard was elected the first postwar mayor of Charleston. When the Radical Republicans took power, he and the entire board of aldermen were removed on February 28, 1868, by General R.S. Canby, occupying military governor. Once the Reconstruction government ended, Gaillard was appointed treasurer of Charleston County, a position that he held until his death in 1889. He founded the Charleston chapter of the Confederate Veterans' Association. Gaillard is buried in Magnolia Cemetery.[84]

William Henry Hendricks risked censure when he became associated with the police department during Republican rule. He was second and afterward first lieutenant of police under Mayor Gaillard, his Confederate commander, and first lieutenant of police under both General Burns and General Cogswell. He was elected chief of police under Mayor G.W. Clark and again under Mayor Pillsbury. He was made deputy marshall by Colonel R.M. Wallace and in 1873 again elected chief of police under Mayor G.I. Cunningham, a position he still held at the time of the 1876 riot. Some held the chief of police accountable, claiming that he protected the blacks who went on the rampage. This did not go down well with responsible citizens of Charleston. By December 1877, roughly two hundred men representing various professional, commercial and industrial interests recommended in a printed pamphlet that Chief of Police Hendricks be retained, stating that they had no "other motive than the welfare of the City and attested their names in appreciation of the valuable services he has rendered in the past." The pamphlet contained a letter of commendation from General Johnson Hagood and another from General Connor, attorney general of South Carolina. A handwritten three-page letter was written on his behalf by P.C. Gaillard, ex-colonel of the Twenty-seventh Regiment and former mayor of Charleston.

Hendricks became chief United States deputy marshal for South Carolina, capping a long and productive career in public service. He died in 1898 and is buried in Magnolia Cemetery.

CHAPTER 14

A Promise Kept

Although Confederate Captain Hendricks kept a war diary when his regiment went north, it is strangely silent about his kindness to a dying Yankee lieutenant. The young man was the son of Judge Halsey R. Wing of Glens Falls, New York. Both of the judge's sons had enlisted in the 118 New York Volunteers when the call to arms came. In 1868, Lieutenant George H. Wing died at Covington, Kentucky, of a disease he contracted while a Confederate prisoner. The other son, Lieutenant Edgar C. Wing, was mortally wounded at Drury's Bluff, Virginia, on April 16, 1864. (According to General Humphreys's *Campaigns of 1864–66*, Drury's Bluff was considered one of the fiercest engagements of the war.)

In the cleanup after the battle, Captain Hendricks found the stricken lieutenant lying among the dead and asked if there was anything that he could do. Knowing that he would soon die, Lieutenant Wing requested that Hendricks return his sword and watch to Judge Wing. He told Hendricks that the sword was the gift from his father, who had desired him to use it bravely and preserve it as a family treasure. He provided his father's address and offered money, which Hendricks refused, saying that Wing might need it at the hospital. Hendricks called for a stretcher and had him sent to the rear. The two parted, never to meet again.

Lieutenant Wing was sent to a field hospital and later put on a boat of Confederate wounded bound for Richmond. While on board, a Mr. Stokes talked to him until late in the evening. Finding that the young man had died before dawn, Stokes made arrangements for Wing's burial, marked the grave site and contacted Judge Wing in Glens Falls. After the war, the judge went south, and with Stokes's assistance, found his son's grave. He brought the body back home for a proper burial in the village cemetery. A monument to Lieutenant Wing was erected in the Glens Falls town square. Because of the solicitude of the two Southern gentlemen, both thought to be Masons, Wing's family cherished "very kindly feelings toward the South."

For safekeeping, Hendricks had sent the sword to his wife in South Carolina. Like most Southern women, Cordrean Ackis Hendricks had already been forced to endure a lot. Her brothers, Richard and James Ackis, had enlisted almost immediately; both fought with Rhett's Battery at Gettysburg. Corporal Richard Ackis's head was shot off on July 3, 1863, and his body remained on the battlefield as the fighting raged around his decapitated corpse. His brother James was more fortunate. After a bullet entered his chin and went through his windpipe, he was carried to a barn with other Confederate wounded and left there for three or four days before enemy scouts came upon them.

Expecting the worst from his captors, Ackis later told the family that he was well treated by the women of Gettysburg who followed the biblical injunction, "return good for evil." He was sent by rail to Baltimore where his "youthful appearance and blood besmirched clothing excited sympathy" from the ladies who attended the wounded. This kind treatment continued when he was sent to a hospital in Chester, Pennsylvania. There he was "lionized as a youthful rebel from the cradle of secession." He recovered from his wounds and was paroled. He was exchanged about a month later and went on to fight with Longstreet until he was once again captured. This time he was held prisoner at Point Lookout, Maryland. Although overcrowded, this prison camp was far better than most. He remained there until hostilities ceased.[85]

Cordrean Hendricks never envisioned herself in a heroic role, but the war changed all that. By the time Lieutenant Wing's sword arrived from Virginia, her husband was a prisoner of war. He was exchanged two months later and went home on leave. He returned to duty just before Christmas, leaving a convalescing wife and an infant less than a week old.

As 1864 ended, General Sherman was amassing a huge army in Georgia. Fearing that Charleston would soon fall, many fled the city. While Captain Hendricks was marching to defend Fort Fisher, his family joined the refugees who ended up in Columbia. Thinking that her family treasures would be safe, Cordrean added Wing's sword, sash and belt to the valuables that she took with her.

On February 16, when reports of the enemy got more menacing, Cordrean decided to bury her treasure. Concerned that the servants would betray her, she waited until everyone was asleep before she crawled on her hands and knees beneath the porch of the house where they were staying. In the pitch-black stillness she used makeshift tools to scrape a hole large enough to conceal a small trunk. She wrapped the sword in a blanket, covered it with oilcloth and placed it in a shallow trench scraped in the earth below the trunk. It was such a difficult task that she asked her fifteen-year-old daughter Manny to help.

As it turned out, the family would have been better off had they remained in Mount Pleasant. Sherman's army sacked and burned Columbia the following day. Afterward, Wing's sword became Manny's personal charge. She kept it hidden, as it would have been a prize for soldiers of either side.

There was a separation for a long time before Captain Hendricks finally returned home. He had been a deputy sheriff before the war and returned to work at the police department. Although he made inquiries about the location of Wing's family, Glens Falls was unknown to people in South Carolina.

In time, two more children were born into the Hendricks family. Manny became a beautiful young woman with large brown eyes, dark hair and a sweet disposition. She married Daniel Sinclair in 1870 and had a daughter who died in infancy.

In 1882, Hendricks received a letter from Captain Louis F. Emilio, one of the white officers in charge of the Fifty-fourth Regiment of Massachusetts Volunteers. After the war, Emilio had taken up the cause of the Fifty-fourth and spent years researching and writing about their experiences. Hendricks had fought at Battery Wagner, and it was only natural that Emilio eventually contacted him. Hendricks had witnessed the gallant Shaw's burial and provided comments for Emilio's book.

Emilio had also spent years trying to trace the effects of Edgar Wing, who had been his personal friend. You can imagine his delight when he received the following from Hendricks: "I have in my keeping a sword and sash, the property of Lieutenant Edgar M. Wing of Glens Falls, N.Y. I also had his watch up to my capture, but of which I was quickly relieved when I was made a prisoner. The sword and sash are in good preservation, and I am anxious to return them to some member of his family. Can you assist me?"

By then Hendricks had given his Confederate uniform and sword to his eldest daughter, along with Lieutenant Wing's sword. Once she had the address, Manny wrote the lieutenant's sister, Angie C. Wing. The two women made arrangements for the transfer, and in time the "lost" sword was finally hung above the library mantel in the Wing mansion in Glens Falls.

Manny invited Angie Wing to visit Mount Pleasant. She was a woman of considerable wealth and according to family tradition, "fell in love with Manny and practically adopted her." The women traveled extensively together. In August 1891, they made arrangements to be in Lake George when the GAR "Post Wing," the old "Adirondack" 118 Irish New York, held its annual reunion.

The event is described in a letter addressed to the editor of the *Tribune*, Lake George, New York. After a speech about how the sword was given to Captain Hendricks and later returned to the Wing family, the article described how a guest of Fernwood Cottage listened to the speech.

She was Mrs. Sinclair, of Charleston, the daughter of Captain Hendricks and the preserver and restorer of this sword. The fact became known to the camp and created interest and feeling. The touching incident and the rare chance coincidences of the heroine's nearness after so many years, to the assembled survivors of the dead lieutenant's comrades had a most tender and melting effect upon the camp.

A campfire council was held that night and it was enthusiastically decided to show in some way the veteran's appreciation of this beautiful fidelity by one who wore the enemy's uniform and followed the enemy's flag. The next morning the veterans of the 118 New York Volunteers… followed by all the veterans of the camp, citizens and Lake George visitors, headed by the Citizen Corps band of Glens Falls, marched to the grounds of Fernwood Cottage, the veterans forming in front of the piazza.

Colonel Cunningham, also of the 118, soon appeared on the piazza with Mrs. Sinclair and fellow-guests of the cottage. He touchingly rehearsed an account of the battle and the story of the sword, and dwelt upon its sweetness and peaceful significance, "like finding a nest full of young birds in an old cannon's mouth, or a blossom clinging to a lightning seared oak"—its present effect on these old soldier hearts and their desire not to break ranks until they had paid their homage and grateful respects to this fair daughter of her manly father. The address was tender, impressive and delicate, and during its delivery the tears not only coursed down the honored lady's cheeks, but brought many a coat sleeve across the eyes of the old veterans. A brief but apt response was made by one of the lady's gentlemen friends, when Mrs. Sinclair was introduced and graciously bowed her acknowledgements [as she received] a vociferous "three times three and a tiger." The veterans then passed by in single file and warmly shook the lady by the hand, while many spoke out, "God bless you" and other tender and respectful salutations indicated the depth of feeling with which these old hearts were struggling. It was such an impressive scene that it was almost solemn in the intense silence of the on-looking crowd.

Mrs. Sinclair was afterward unanimously elected an honorary member of the Veterans' association and presented with the badges of the association and of the 118 New York Volunteers, and later a photograph of the veterans formed in a semi-circle with this lady and her special friends in their midst, was taken and christened "The Angel of Peace."[86]

CHAPTER 15

A Confederate Heroine

War quickly changed the face of Charleston. The blockade stranglehold began to take effect, and communications with the war front were so poor that often families had little news of their absent loved ones. By May 1862, there were many refugees. Upcountry towns were overcrowded, and prices were exorbitant. With the men away at war, only those over- or underage were left to plant crops. Often Confederate money was refused by farmers who preferred to hoard their provisions rather than sell them for worthless money.

In those uncertain times, survival was left to the women. They helped the cause by making clothes for the soldiers, nursing the wounded and keeping the home fires burning under extremely difficult circumstances. Some Confederate women were well known, others have faded into obscurity, but their unwavering support was as important as any victory in battle.

In 1903, the Daughters of the Confederacy published *South Carolina Women in the Confederacy* with the stated purpose of presenting the character and services of women during the war. The state legislature appropriated $500 to purchase three hundred books to be placed in the state's public schools. Opposite the title page is the picture of Mrs. Amarinthia Yates Snowden, whose philanthropic works so inspired the South Carolina Legislature that in 1917 the General Assembly and the United Daughters of the Confederacy erected a marble memorial tablet in her honor in the Statehouse rotunda. Some of her charitable works still exist in Charleston.

Mary Amarinthia Yates was born in Charleston in 1819, the daughter of Joseph and Elizabeth Ann Saylor Yates. Her father died when she was

Amarinthia Yates Snowden. *Courtesy The Confederate Home, Charleston, South Carolina.*

eighteen months old, and her mother moved her young family to Philadelphia so that her older children could be educated in a manner suitable to their social status.

When the family later returned to Charleston, Miss Yates attended Madame Talvande's exclusive finishing school in the famous "Sword Gates" house at 32 Legare Street. She completed her formal education at the state's most prestigious girls' school, Dr. Elias Marks's Academy in Barhamville,

"Pupils at their studies on board the *Lodebar*."(*Harper's Weekly*, December 8, 1860.) *Courtesy Charleston Museum, Charleston, South Carolina.*

near Columbia. (One of her classmates at Barhamville was Ann Pamela Cunningham, who organized the Mount Vernon Preservation Society and worked to have it registered as a national monument.)

Miss Yates's first humanitarian work was with her brother, the Reverend William B. Yates, pastor of the Mariners Church. Reverend Yates founded the "School Ship Lodebar" mission to rehabilitate "homeless" sailors by sponsoring them to learn discipline and literacy aboard a sailing ship.

Miss Yates had known John C. Calhoun personally and greatly admired him. In 1854, she gathered ten women in her mother's drawing room at 15 Church Street and organized the Ladies Calhoun Memorial Association (LCMA); its mission was to erect a monument honoring

Major General William T. Sherman. *Library of Congress.*

the national contributions of John C. Calhoun. They raised $40,000, much of it from two benefit bazaars, a highly unusual activity for antebellum Southern women. Within four years, the LCMA had obtained support of the local Gentlemen's Committee dedicated to the same purpose.

The cornerstone was laid at Marion Square on June 28, 1858, anniversary of the patriots' stunning victory at Fort Moultrie during the Revolution. A cannonball that had been recovered from the harbor and was supposed to have been used in the famous battle, a case containing a banner carried in Calhoun's funeral procession, $100 in Continental money, a lock of Calhoun's hair and lists of various cabinets since the Revolution were placed in the monument's cavity.

Before the monument's completion, war diverted attention to more pressing needs. The LCMA resolved to finish it once peace was restored. In 1862, members of the LCMA had a fair to help raise money for a ship to help counter the effects of the blockade.

During the war, there was no Red Cross to help care for the soldiers. Mrs. Snowden was one of the founding officers of the Soldiers' Relief Association of Charleston; they raised money, clothed and partially fed the Confederate army. Mrs. Snowden volunteered as a nurse at South Carolina hospitals. After the second battle of Manassas (August 1862), accompanied by her husband, she traveled to Virginia to nurse the wounded, ministering to 180 South Carolinians lying on Academy Hill as well as those who were fortunate enough to be housed nearby.

January 1865 found Mrs. Snowden refugeeing in Columbia. She commandeered the South Carolina State House for a last-ditch effort to raise money for the Confederacy. The Great Bazaar raised $350,000. Its success was attributed, in part, to Mrs. Snowden's being given authority to import wine and liquor through the blockade when space was available. (Some of the spirits were sent on to aid wounded Confederate soldiers at Chimborazo Hospital in Richmond.)

A Confederate Heroine

When Sherman made his fateful march to Columbia, Mrs. Snowden wrote the general requesting that he receive her and her entourage. They had met in 1850 when Sherman had escorted Miss Yates to wedding festivities in Charleston. Miss Yates was then a beautiful, intelligent and popular young woman who had refused many suitors before her marriage to Dr. William Snowden in 1857. Even after years of war, Sherman remembered her fondly and extended every courtesy to her and her charges.

As LCMA treasurer, Mrs. Snowden was responsible for protecting its remaining funds, which had been invested in U.S. Bonds. She and her sister had secretly quilted the bonds, worth about $39,000, into Mrs. Snowden's petticoat, a story that has been inscribed on the Calhoun Monument. No one suspected that the resourceful Mrs. Snowden carried $39,000 of bonds on her person while she was protected by General Sherman.

After the burning of Columbia, Mrs. Snowden received special permission to care for Confederate prisoners held in the South Carolina College. Her slaves were given their freedom but elected to remain with their mistress when she pointed out the disagreeable tasks that were allotted freedmen. She pensioned her servants the rest of their lives.

Since the Battle of Secessionville, Confederate dead had been buried in Magnolia Cemetery. In 1866, Mrs. Snowden organized the Ladies' Memorial Association. Plans were made for headstones. The South Carolina Legislature contributed $1,000 and agreed to donate the granite and marble left over from the construction of the State House. Before the Ladies' Memorial Association could get the stone transported to Charleston, however, control of the government had shifted to the Reconstruction Republicans. Mrs. Snowden went to Columbia anyway and, through her efforts and the threat of legal action, returned with enough material to cut more than eight hundred headstones. A granite monument was completed in 1872; a bronze Confederate soldier was placed on top in 1880. Both she and Reverend Ellison Capers were present at the dedication in the Confederate cemetery. (On the base of the monument is a tablet inscribed to the memory of Mrs. Snowden.)

After Southern forces surrendered, the resolute matron traveled from battlefield to battlefield making arrangements to bring home the dead. Through the generosity of Moses Cohen Mordecai, a wealthy Jewish merchant who lived at 69 Meeting Street, Mrs. Snowden was able to travel to Gettysburg in 1871 to locate Confederate graves. What she found were greedy farmers who wanted to be compensated for the bones. Once again, Mrs. Snowden used her powers of persuasion and contracted to pay $3.25 for each box of bones shipped to Charleston. (Mordecai was personally opposed to secession but supported the Confederacy as a blockade runner; he lost his fortune during the conflict and moved to Baltimore after the war.)

Mrs. Snowden's good works were not confined to war-related activities. On August 12, 1867, at a meeting of nine women and the Reverend Charles Stuart Vedder, of the Huguenot Church, the Home for the Mothers, Widows and Daughters of Confederate Soldiers was established as a living memorial to the soldiers of the Confederacy. The available funds were one dollar given by a widow living in a charitable institution in Baltimore and enough money to pay one year's rent at the Old Carolina Hotel (now the Confederate Home at 60–64 Broad Street). To raise the money for the first year's rent, Mrs. Snowden, then a widow, and her widowed sister Isabella S. Snowden mortgaged their lovely Church Street home that their father had built in 1842. The sisters and eight other women formed a Board of Control and in 1874 purchased the building for $12,000. Through the help of the South Carolina legislature, two years later they acquired the lot on the east. (The Repository of the Charleston Bible Society was purchased in 1908.)

A school, known as the Confederate College, was added to educate Confederate daughters. The ladies tried to have the endowment for the Calhoun Monument transferred from the Calhoun Monument Association. Certain powerful men blocked the transfer, particularly Thomas Green Clemson, who wanted the money for a state college he hoped to establish on Calhoun's old estate, which he named for himself instead of Calhoun.

Mrs. Snowden died at home in 1898. Many Confederate veterans walked in the funeral procession for the services held at the Huguenot Church. She is buried at Magnolia Cemetary.[87]

Dr. and Mrs. Snowden had two children: Yates Snowden, a history professor at the University of South Carolina, and a daughter who taught at the Confederate College her mother had founded.

CHAPTER 16

The Irrepressible Levy Sisters

T he earliest known reference to a Jew in the Charles Towne colony
was in 1695, and within fifty years, Jewish colonists were sufficiently
numerous to organize a congregation. By 1794, they dedicated a beautifully
proportioned synagogue building described as the largest in the United
States. In the early 1800s, Charleston's Jewish community was the largest in
North America, and they commonly referred to the city as "our Jerusalem."

Some ten thousand Jews served in the Civil War, with about one-third
fighting for the Confederate cause. The most famous Southern Jew of the
nineteenth century was Judah Philip Benjamin. Born in the West Indies in
1811, Judah Benjamin immigrated with his family and grew up in Charleston.
He moved to New Orleans and later served in the Confederate Cabinet
until the Confederacy collapsed, causing him to flee the country. Abraham
Myers, a West Point graduate and classmate of Robert E. Lee, served as the
Confederate Quartermaster General.

Among Charleston Jews who supported the Confederacy were General
E.W. Moise and Dr. Marx E. Choen. Moses Mordecai was a blockade runner
who gave generously to the Confederacy. In addition, numerous Charleston
Jews fought valiantly alongside their gentile countrymen. But perhaps it is
two daughters of Jacob Clavius Levy and Phoebe Yates Levy whom history
remembers best.

Levy was the son of Polish immigrants. He married Phoebe Yates,
a British actress whom he met while visiting Liverpool as a young man.
After their marriage, the couple moved to 26 Society Street in Charleston
where Levy operated a successful mercantile establishment. He was director

of the Union Insurance Company (1830–40), a delegate to the Knoxville Railroad Convention in 1836 and a member of the Charleston Chamber of Commerce from 1841 to 1847. Politically, he was a Union Democrat who opposed nullification and secession. The family was prominent in the Kahal Kadosh Beth Elohim (Holy Congregation House of God) Synagogue and mingled with the city's elite. Mrs. Levy continued to enjoy her acting career in the Charleston theatre. In 1848, after financial reversals, the Levys moved to Savannah.

When the war started, it was predictable that the Levys' son, Samuel Yates Levy, would serve as a major in the Georgia infantry. He was captured and imprisoned in 1864 on Johnson's Island in Ohio. He no doubt fought gallantly before his capture, but his exploits pale before those of his sisters.[88]

EUGENIA LEVY PHILLIPS—SPY AND PROVOCATEUR

One of six daughters, Eugenia Levy was born in Charleston in 1820. When Eugenia was sixteen, she married Philip Phillips, a prominent Jewish lawyer who stood firmly against nullification in the nullification crisis and went on to serve in the South Carolina legislature from 1834 to 1835. When his term was over, the couple moved to Mobile and lived there for the next eighteen years. Phillips was an attorney for the Bank of Mobile and became an established lawyer, handling several hundred cases a year. While in Mobile, the couple had seven children. (Two more sons were born after the family moved to Washington, D.C.)

A political activist, Phillips was chairman of the Alabama Democratic Party and served two terms in the state legislature before being elected to the U.S. Congress in 1853. At a salary half of what he had made before, Phillips declined reelection and set up a lucrative private practice handling Supreme Court cases in Washington. Their privileged background made it possible for them to enjoy Washington's stimulating social life. Among Philip Phillips's friends were Edwin M. Stanton (James Buchanan's lame duck attorney general and Lincoln's secretary of war), associate Supreme Court justice James M. Wayne and Maryland congressman Reverdy Johnson.

While her husband supported the North, Eugenia Phillips was an outspoken Southern sympathizer, something that quickly got her into trouble after the war started. In her own words, "Southern women gave free expression to the feelings which habit had made but second nature, and spoke of their hatred and determination to sustain their rights by encouraging in their husbands, sons, and fathers every resistance to tyranny exhibited by the Republicans."[89]

Her unbridled tongue caused her to be suspected of being a member of a Confederate spy ring, and in August 1861, Union soldiers entered the Phillips home. Although the troops found no evidence of treason, everyone was placed under house arrest. Eugenia Phillips, her sister Martha Levy and two of her daughters were imprisoned in the filthy attic of another suspected Confederate spy, Rose O'Neal Greenhow, popularly known as "Rebel Rose."

Fortunately, Edwin M. Stanton, then Lincoln's secretary of war, intervened, and the Phillips women were released with the understanding that they would move south. Phillips was forced to auction off everything in his house and, with the help of General Winfield Scott, was permitted to take $5,000 with him when he and his family traveled to Richmond. While there, Eugenia gave Jefferson Davis military maps and intelligence from Mrs. Greenhow that she had managed to smuggle out of Washington.

The Phillips family continued south, stopping in Charleston, where they enjoyed breakfast with John Slidell and James Mason of the Trent Affair, before proceeding to New Orleans. Phillips hoped to set up another law practice, but with a war in progress, the law business was dead. Instead of being far away from hostilities, they soon discovered that New Orleans was unable to defend itself.

Once the Union fleet broke through, Confederate soldiers burned boats, bales of cotton, molasses and other items of commercial value lest they fall in the hands of the enemy. Amid the conflagration and destruction, News Orleans surrendered to General Benjamin "Beast" Butler on April 29, 1862. He treated the city to rigorous martial law and imprisoned a large number of uncooperative citizens. International furor over some of his policies hastened his removal from command of the Department of the Gulf; he was relieved on December 17, 1862, though the scars left by his regime lingered for decades.

The women of New Orleans treated the occupying soldiers so contemptuously that on May 15, 1862, Butler issued "The Women's Order." It read: "As the officers and soldiers of the United States have been subjected to repeated insults from the women (calling themselves ladies) of New Orleans, in return for the most scrupulous non-interference and courtesy on our part, it is ordered, that hereafter, when any female shall, by word, gesture, or movement, insult or show contempt for any officer or soldier of the United States, she shall be regarded and held liable to be treated as a woman of the town plying her avocation," i.e., a common prostitute. This proclamation evoked protests not only both in the North and South but also England and France.

Some weeks later, there was a funeral of a Union officer, and the citizens of New Orleans were informed that the procession would pass through the French Quarter. As they passed under Eugenia Phillips's balcony, she was heard laughing. When called to task by General Butler, she later claimed that she was hosting a children's party and was laughing at their antics. The general was enraged at her defiance and had her arrested and unceremoniously exiled to Ship Island, Mississippi, a desolate barrier island in the Gulf of Mexico. Permitted to

Major General Benjamin F. "Beast" Butler. *Courtesy Library of Congress.*

take only her maid for company, Phillips spent a miserable summer fighting insects, heat, poor food and horrible accommodations.

Butler's treatment of Eugenia Phillips violated the code of Southern chivalry, and news of her imprisonment spread throughout the South. She quickly became a symbol of injustice, and her widely circulated patriotic letters from Ship Island turned her into an overnight Southern heroine. The Spartan conditions caused her health to fail, and she was released three months later at the intervention of her husband and some of his Washington friends.

Afterward, the Phillipses were greeted with cheers whenever they appeared in public, and crowds made pilgrimages to their home. Eugenia Phillips became an embarrassment to Butler, and the family was forced to move back into Confederate territory. They eventually landed in La Grange, Georgia, where they spent the remainder of the war.

By 1867, Philip Phillips was able to return to Washington, where he gained respect for the way he handled cases before the Supreme Court. He died in 1884. Eugenia Phillips later wrote "Journal of Mrs. Eugenia Phillips: 1861–1862." She died in 1902.[90]

PHOEBE YATES LEVY PEMBER
TRAILBLAZING CONFEDERATE NURSE

Born in 1823, Phoebe Yates Levy was the fourth child in the Levy household. Little is known about her youth. At age twenty-seven, she married Thomas Noyes Pember, a Bostonian and a gentile. Before Thomas Pember's untimely death, the couple lived in Richmond for a time and became friends with the city's society. When Thomas developed tuberculosis, the couple moved farther south. In 1861, Thomas Pember died in Aiken, South Carolina.

Left childless, the young widow went to live with her parents who had fled to Marietta to escape the war. Unhappy at home because of difficulties with her father, she decided to make a contribution to the war effort. She found that opportunity through the Matron Law, legislation enacted in 1862 to give administrative responsibility to women in order to free men for military service.

Many decried the "petticoat government" that emerged in Richmond. Educated, upper-class women raised money for the army and processed the government's paperwork, printed currency and sorted mail. Working class and immigrant women manufactured cartridges and shells, while black women, both enslaved and free, did unskilled work in factories and military hospitals.

While in Richmond, Phoebe Pember had become friends with the wife of the Confederate secretary of war, Mrs. George Randolph. Through that connection, she was offered a position as the first female administrator at Chimborazo Military Hospital, a sprawling complex on the outskirts of Richmond. Once the largest hospital in the world, it had 150 single-story wards, each thirty feet wide and one hundred feet long.

Being a hospital administrator was an unusual job for a woman at a time when all nursing was done by men. Although she had no formal training, the young widow felt that years of caring for her sickly husband had qualified her for the job. In a letter to her sister Eugenia Phillips, she admitted she was a little anxious about her decision: "You may imagine how frightened and nervous I feel concerning the step I am about to take and how important in this small way it will be to me, for I have too much common sense to underrate what I am giving up." In the same letter she also wrote that she was proud to have entire charge of her department. [91]

The challenges began almost immediately. When the new matron arrived, she overheard a surgeon mutter that "one of them had come." Dr. James McCaw, the surgeon-in-charge, had made no preparations for female nurses, so she set to work converting a vacant building into her own quarters, including an office, parlor, laundry area, pantry and kitchen. Not knowing exactly

Phoebe Yates Levy Pember. *Courtesy* Charleston Mercury, *Charleston, South Carolina.*

what her responsibilities were, Pember started her employment by cleaning an unused kitchen and preparing chicken soup for the patients. When Dr. McCaw discovered her peeling potatoes, he saw that she was assigned a full staff (assistant matron, cooks, bakers and two laborers for menial tasks).

In the midst of limited personnel, unsanitary conditions and shortages of medicine, food and equipment, Pember did everything humanly possible to alleviate the suffering of the wounded and quickly earned the respect of Richmond society. She administered medication, assisted surgeons and cared for patients, often providing comfort to the dying men by writing letters home, reading stories, playing cards and praying with her patients.

Her patients taught her about courage. "No words can do justice to the uncomplaining nature of the Southern soldier," she later wrote. "Day after day, whether lying wasted by disease or burning up with fever, torn with wounds or sinking from debility, a groan was seldom heard."[92]

The most difficult encounter at Chimborazo was with a young soldier named Fisher. After months of nursing a severe hip wound, he had turned over in bed and cried out in severe pain. Discovering that a splintered bone had severed one of his arteries, Pember staunched the gushing blood with her finger and summoned a surgeon who looked at the wound and shook his head sadly. Fisher turned his questioning eyes upon Pember.

"How long can I live," he asked. "Only as long as I keep my finger on this artery." A pause ensued. She wrote later, "God alone knew what thoughts hurried through that heart and brain, called so unexpectedly from all earthly hopes and ties. He broke the silence at last. 'You can let go.'" But she could not. The horror of the situation overcame her, and for the only time at Chimborazo, she fainted.[93]

The new administrator was flooded with countless petty requests from her staff, but her all-consuming passion was caring for the sick, wounded and dying. At times the responsibilities were overwhelming, and she found respite by renting an overpriced room in town and occasionally visiting with friends.

Not long after her employment, "wars of the whiskey barrel" started. Each hospital division received a monthly barrel of medicinal whiskey, except the female matron, whose barrel remained at the dispensary under the guardianship of an apothecary who jealously guarded the right to dole out its contents. Under his watch, whiskey was pilfered and gone before her ward was entitled to more. The strong-willed matron eventually obtained jurisdiction of her ward's monthly whiskey ration, but resentments among the male doctors and nurses lingered.

The situation might have continued through the war had patients not complained about the lack of stimulants. The indomitable Pember marched over to the ward and confronted them. Some patients hinted that several champagne bottles were hidden behind a vacant bed and could easily be spirited away in the night. Incensed, she tracked down the ward master, but he indicated that another party was guilty. An hour later, the ward surgeon accosted her and swore that his ward master did not drink. She replied, "I know he does not, and I also know who does." When the doctor's fiery flush revealed him as the true culprit, Pember threatened to take the matter to the proper authorities and have him sent to the field. The drunken doctor tried to discredit her, but it was the surgeon who soon left Chimborazo, never to return.

The final confrontation over the whiskey barrel was the Monday after the Confederates evacuated Richmond. After a particularly exhausting day, Pember had collapsed onto her straw mattress. Suddenly, she was awakened by a threatening mob that had broken into her quarters. The men were malingerers who were scornfully referred to as "hospital rats." The ringleader was a long-time hospital malcontent named Wilson.

He ordered his men to pick up the barrel, but they were not accustomed to defying the self-willed socialite matron and backed off. Pember stepped between her adversary and the whiskey barrel. She watched as Wilson's "fierce temper blazed up in his face, and catching me roughly by the shoulder, he called me a name that a decent woman seldom hears and even a wicked one resents." As he was about to shove her out of the way, he heard the telltale sound of a pistol being cocked beneath the folds of the matron's skirt. She advised him to leave and warned, "If one bullet is lost, there are five more ready, and the room is too small for even a woman to miss six times."

Wilson backed off threatening, "You think yourself very brave now, but wait an hour; perhaps others may have pistols too, and you won't have it entirely your way after all." After the encounter, Pember nailed the head of a flour barrel across the back door and sat down on the whiskey barrel, the pistol within easy reach. The men did not return.[94]

Although the hospital staff hastily left before the Federal authorities took over Chimborazo, Matron Pember remained behind, writing in her memoirs that duty prompted her to remain with the sick, on the ground that "no general ever deserts his troops." The faithful Pember remained on duty until all her patients had convalesced, died or been taken to another hospital.

Then it was over, and she suddenly found herself alone in an occupied city with only a box of useless Confederate money and a silver ten-cent piece. Laughing at her lot, she used her meager funds to purchase a box of matches and five coconut cakes.

Afterward, Pember returned to Savannah and traveled extensively. In 1879, she published *A Southern Woman's Story: Life in Confederate Richmond*, detailing hardships encountered in Richmond and the Chimborazo Military Hospital. In her last years, she wrote for the popular *Atlantic Monthly* and *Harper's Weekly*; she was frequently honored by Confederate organizations. She lived with her niece in Pittsburgh and died of breast cancer in 1913. Phoebe Pember was buried next to her husband in Laurel Grove Cemetery in Savannah, Georgia.

Today, historians consider *A Southern Woman's Story* the finest first-person account of life inside a Confederate hospital and a landmark in women's history. Through her efforts and those of other female nurses, Phoebe Pember changed popular opinion about nursing and established a model for future generations. In 1995, Nurse Pember's portrait appeared on a sheet of twenty stamps when the U.S. Postal Service commemorated important persons and events of the Civil War. In Charleston, Phoebe Pember's childhood home at 26 Society is now a tony bed and breakfast. Chimborazo houses the Confederate Medical Museum and is part of the Richmond National Battlefield Park.[95]

CHAPTER 17

Evacuation and Occupation

Following General William Tecumseh Sherman's infamous "March to the Sea" in late 1864, Union soldiers entered Savannah and began staging sixty thousand troops for the invasion of South Carolina. The assembled forces consisted of the Fourteenth, Fifteenth, Seventeenth and Twentieth Army Corps plus four thousand cavalry. To split up the Confederates defending South Carolina, Sherman's strategy was to confuse General Beauregard as long as possible about whether the armies would head to Charleston or Columbia.

Troops in the Lowcountry were under the command of Lieutenant General William J. Hardee, a seasoned veteran who had been transferred from the Army of Tennessee. Known as "Old Reliable," Hardee commanded approximately twelve thousand untested coastal artillerymen and garrison troops. To augment this, Lee sent a brigade of South Carolina infantrymen, known throughout the war as "Kershaw's Brigade," named in honor of its original commander, Brigadier General Joseph Brevard Kershaw from Camden. In 1865, it was commanded by Brigadier General John Doby Kennedy, also of Camden. By the time the brigade returned to Charleston, it had already served in the major battles of Northern Virginia and the Wilderness campaign and had fought in the Shenandoah Valley, Maryland and Gettysburg.

Kershaw's Brigade arrived in Charleston on the Savannah and Charleston rail line. The first night that they were back in town, hundreds of barrels of whiskey were rolled out into the street, where happy soldiers knocked out the barrel heads and either "confiscated" the whiskey or allowed it to run in the streets to keep it from falling into the hands of the enemy.

Convinced that their city was Sherman's objective, Charlestonians sent their valuables and important papers to Columbia for safekeeping. Those who had the means had already sought refuge elsewhere.

Once Sherman's army neared Orangeburg, Beauregard became concerned that they would capture the Northeastern Railroad, the last railroad still in Confederate hands. Not wanting his troops trapped in Charleston, Hardee chose to evacuate and ordered withdrawal from the outlying batteries with the soldiers in the city to follow. Neighboring planters sent their young women into Charleston hoping they would be safe from molestation by Sherman's men.

The departing soldiers were to rendezvous at St. Stephen. Some were fortunate enough to hitch a ride on the trains leaving Charleston, although they were so crowded that some rode on top of the cars in a driving rain. Others were forced to march. When the exhausted soldiers began arriving in St. Stephen, some forty miles distant, so many had deserted en route that some artillery companies were almost disbanded due to loss of men.[96]

Meanwhile, after 567 days of siege, Charleston fell to Union troops. On February 18, Mayor Charles MacBeth surrendered the city to General Alexander Schimmelfenning. Lee C. Harby provides a contemporary civilian perspective:

For days previous to February 18th, stores were being removed and ammunition sent away with each successive body of men who left the city. On the 16th, cotton was piled on the public square and burned, that it might not enrich the enemy. The rice—tens of thousands of bushels—at Lucas' Mill was set on fire. On the 17th, the Northeastern Depot, where a large amount of military stores had been collected and abandoned, was thronged with a motley crowd of people, who bore away to their homes provisions of every kind. As the day wore on, explosions were heard on every side; the gunboats Charleston and Chicora were blown up at their wharves; the "big gun" at the corner of South and East Battery was exploded, and tore out the windows and doors and shattered the roof and piazzas of Mr. Louis DeSaussure's residence, at the opposite corner. The night which followed was a fearful one; no one slept; few went to bed. Fires started everywhere, and there were only negroes to put them out. They knew the end had come; that the white men had gone or were going, and that the city was helpless and expecting its foe on the morrow. Yet, be it said to their honor, not a case of

"Sherman's march through South Carolina—Advance of McPhersonville." (*Harper's Weekly*, February 1, 1865) *Courtesy Charleston Museum, Charleston, South Carolina.*

"Sherman's march through South Carolina—Burning from McPhersonville." (*Harper's Weekly*, February 1, 1865) *Courtesy Charleston Museum, Charleston, South Carolina.*

outrage or violence disgraced their record that night. They hauled the engines about to the tune and words of "Massa run away; nigger stay at home," but they put out the fires, and helped the whites, and did their duty manfully.

Late in the night of the 17th, the Palmetto State, the gunboat that the ladies built, was blown up at the Gas Company's Wharf, where she lay. Women who had worked and striven and contributed to its building stood at their windows and viewed the flames from the burning boat color the sky, and lo! as the last detonation sounded, the smoke arose and, upon the red glare of the heavens, formed a palmetto tree, perfect and fair, that stood out against the sky, then wavered and broke apart as we watched it through our tears, then crumbled into wreck and ruin and was lost in the darkness and gloom!...

It was a terrible, heart-breaking, awful night. The men who were garrisoning Sumter had come over in their small boats, bringing their flags. In the early morning of the 18th, they were gathered in the city on the wharf, and there they cast themselves down on the earth and wept aloud. Some prayed; some cursed; all said they would rather have died in the fort they had so long defended than have her ramparts desecrated by the invader's tread.

About eight o'clock in the morning of the 18th, a terrible accident occurred through the carelessness of boys who went back and forth from the Northeastern Depot stores, carrying powder in their hands and throwing it upon the burning cotton in the yard. The place was crowded with plunderers, people of all sorts and conditions, and as the powder trickled through their fingers, the boys unconsciously laid a train from the burning mass to the depot. There was a fearful explosion, and the place was torn to atoms; a hundred and fifty persons were killed, and about two hundred wounded; but no one had time to concern himself with it—the flames spread, and soon the fire was raging down the entire length of Alexander Street, wiping out some of the handsomest residences in the city.

All day on the 17th, the evacuation of our troops had proceeded. On the 18th, at ten o'clock, on Meeting street, near Anne, the last body of armed Confederates we were ever to see said good-bye to the weeping women who pressed around them. Yet, even then, some laughed and jested, for, God pity us, we were hopeful still, and they were brave, and we could not think that the end had really come...

Over the west side of Charleston, in the vicinity of the Arsenal, every inhabitant of the neighborhood had fled, terror-stricken, from their homes, to the Christ Church Chapel, up Rutledge Avenue. The warning had gone out that a train of powder had been laid, and a slow match applied, and that the magazine and building would be blown up. They set wide open

Ruins of the North Eastern Railroad once located near the Cooper River waterfront. Chartered in 1851, the railroad opened in 1856 and was wholly dependent on local traffic in a thinly populated agricultural region of the state. It ran from Charleston north to the Wilmington & Manchester Railroad at Florence. *Library of Congress.*

every door, and raised every window in their homes, then fled for their lives. In dread they listened for the explosion that would doubtless have left them homeless. The minutes passed, but no detonation was heard; all was still. Soon came another messenger, crying that the enemy were in the city, and the arsenal was saved; the Federals had hurried to take possession of it, and were just in time, it was said, to extinguish the fuse.

But another danger threatened, for they were told that all unoccupied houses would be immediately taken possession of by the troops. Back rushed the

"Marching on!—the Fifty-fifth Massachusetts Colored Regiment singing John Brown's March in the Streets of Charleston." (*Harper's Weekly*, February 21, 1865.) *Courtesy Charleston Museum, Charleston, South Carolina.*

harrassed crowd of women, children, and servants, to go to their homes, close windows, lock doors, and await in dread what would be next.

That day (Saturday) passed without event, but Sunday ushered in an era of outrages. They were mostly negro troops, under the command of Lieutenant-Colonel Bennett, who entered Charleston, and these, on the 19th, were permitted to go and liberate their "brothers in bondage." They entered everywhere; they thrust themselves into the apartments of delicate women, cursing and raving at them, and ordering them to give up the slaves they were "concealing." In the meantime, the house negroes, shaking with fear came out from wheresoever they were, and meekly allowed themselves to be escorted off.

Then began the new life for the women of Charleston—the life of service to family necessities. They did their whole duty in that sphere, cheerfully and well, in spite of the traditions and training of generations of gentlewomen. They cooked, swept, and scrubbed; they split wood, fed horses, milked and watered the cattle, and took upon themselves the duties of not only the servants of the family, while filling their own places, but they had to be the men of the household as well, for some slept on the battlefields, some in the burying grounds of distant prisons, and others were incapacitated by sickness and wounds, and came home to be cared for, and be a precious, loved, but additional burden, upon the devoted women who were then, and for long years after, the mainstay of the home.

But the young boys, bless them! of ten, twelve, fourteen, were a comfort indeed. They were everywhere, lending a helping hand to this old lady or splitting wood and carrying water for some girl who had not yet learned how to handle an axe or lift a heavy bucket; going "down town" on many an errand, when women shrank from being in the crowded streets, jostled by the negro soldiery. And how we valued them! how glad we were to save for them a nice tid-bit, a dainty cake, a part of whatever we had that was best! We were grateful to them, and tried to show it.

The negroes came straggling back after some days; but they did not stay. There was no money to pay them regular wages, and their uniformed friends had taught them that to work without a compensation in money was still to be in slavery. Some very few were fond enough of their "white people" to stay by the children they had helped raise; a good many lingered for a month or two, and then went off to some one who could pay them well. No one blamed them for that: every human being seeks to better his condition. There were some cases of bad behavior, but those were comparatively few.

It was the negro soldiery and their white brethren in arms who committed the dastardly outrages but too common in the city. One poor lady with a babe but two or three days old was turned out of her bed, her mattresses and blankets taken, her house looted, and she was sent out into the street to seek succor. Some kind friend took her in and cared for her; but mother and child both died. That was but one instance; there were many others as dreadful. Here is one in lighter vein: Mrs. Laura Postell Geddings wrote to a friend that she had just come out of the kitchen, where she had been cooking Dr. Geddings' supper, while her maid, who had possessed herself of her mistress' best silk gown, sat down in her parlor and entertained the Yankee officers![97]

On February 22, the United States flag was raised once again over Fort Sumter, and later in the day Rear Admiral John Dahlgren took official possession of the burning, ruined city. When news reached Washington, President Lincoln appointed the anniversary of the fall of Fort Sumter (April 14) for a victorious flag-raising ceremony.

By then the war had ended, for all practical purposes. On April 9, General Robert E. Lee surrendered at Appomattox Courthouse. General Grant, in an

Major Robert Anderson (Brevet Major General at the time of the flag raising). *Library of Congress.*

Crowd inside Fort Sumter awaiting the flag-raising ceremony. *Library of Congress.*

untraditional gesture, allowed General Lee to keep his handsome officer's sabre and his officers were permitted to keep their side arms and private horses. On April 12, the Army of Northern Virginia disbanded. It was a poignant moment in history. General Joshua Lawrence Chamberlain, who was later awarded the Medal of Honor for defending Little Round Top at Gettysburg, was selected to preside at the formal surrender. As the downcast parade of Confederate soldiers marched to surrender their arms and colors, Chamberlain, on his own initiative, ordered his men to come to attention as a show of respect, a military courtesy that was deeply appreciated by the defeated warriors.

Boats festooned with flags witnessed the flag-raising ceremony. *Library of Congress.*

Back in South Carolina, Brevet Major General Robert Anderson had triumphantly returned to Charleston. On April 14, amid much pomp and circumstance, Anderson raised the same flag that had been lowered at Fort Sumter four years earlier. The ceremony had been meticulously planned by Secretary Stanton. When the banner reached the top of the flagstaff, there was a salute by six guns at Fort Sumter that was responded to by all the batteries that took part in the bombardment in 1861.

Three thousand African Americans attended, including Robert Smalls and the son of Denmark Vesey, who had been executed for his part in a slave insurrection decades earlier. Leading Abolitionists attended, among them

Henry Ward Beecher and William Lloyd Garrison. In addition, boats gaily festooned with flags were anchored nearby to accommodate spectators who came to witness the historic celebration.

That evening there was a ball, supper and fireworks. Anderson made a heartfelt toast to the president of the United States. On that same evening, Abraham Lincoln was assassinated in Washington.

With the Confederacy's star quickly dimming, other commanders soon laid down their arms. General Joseph E. Johnston's army in North Carolina surrendered to Sherman on April 26, and by June all Confederate land forces had surrendered.

Once hostilities ended, the defeated had to learn to live in a new world where cotton wasn't king. South Carolina was one of three states occupied by United States troops until 1877. The state constitution was rewritten and a new ruling class emerged during Reconstruction occupation.

"Citizens of Charleston, S.C., taking the Oath of Allegiance.—from a sketch by our Special Artist." (*Leslie's Illustrated*, April 15, 1865.) *Courtesy Charleston Museum, Charleston, South Carolina.*

To keep their property, former Confederates had to swear an oath of allegiance to the United States. Returning soldiers had to adjust to the challenges of surviving in a land where the entire economy had been obliterated.

The economic collapse was made worse because a host of adventurers flocked south to make money out of the opportunities opened up by the conquerors. Books have been written about the harsh years of Reconstruction and the punitive measures that were enforced by a government that became so vindictive that even adherents deserted its radical leaders.

The seeds planted by the Nullifiers had borne their bitter fruit. Secession was an utter failure, and memories of the privations suffered by the once-ruling oligarchy in South Carolina were perpetuated for generations.

The Reverend Dr. A. Toomer Porter witnessed the signing of the Ordinance of Secession and wrote its sad epitaph:

> *Then each went up and signed the paper, and the deed was done, which cost millions and millions of money, tens of thousands of lives, destruction of cities and villages, plantations and farms, the emancipation of five millions of African slaves, the entire upheaval of society, the impoverishment of a nation; and let loose a demoralization which has left its impress on the whole land, North and South. It was a deed which made the North rich and the South poor, and has made Southern life one great struggle from that day to this* [1897].

CHAPTER 18

Cameos

PIERRE GUSTAVE TOUTANT BEAUREGARD

1818–1823

Beauregard was born to an aristocratic Louisiana family. He graduated second in his class at the Unites States Military Academy and served with distinction in the Mexican-American War under General Winfield Scott. Beauregard was appointed superintendent of West Point for only five days before it was revoked when Louisiana seceded from the Union. The South's first brigadier general, Beauregard became a national hero for the way he commanded the defenses of Charleston. His reputation increased after the Confederate victory at the first battle of Manassas. After a command in the Western Theatre, he returned to Charleston in 1863. Because the port remained open until evacuation, Beauregard was a hero to Charlestonians. In appreciation, a full-length portrait hangs outside the chambers of Charleston City Hall, while another hangs inside the council chambers; a monument to Beauregard was erected in Washington Park in 1904. (Beauregard rarely used his first name and signed correspondence G.T. Beauregard.)

Barnard Elliott Bee
1823–1861

The son of Colonel Barnard Elliott Bee Sr. and the grandson of Thomas Bee, first Federal judge of South Carolina, Barnard Elliot Bee graduated from the United States Military Academy in 1845. In 1847, he took part in the siege of Vera Cruz and the storming of Cerro Gordo; he fought at Contreras, Churubusco, Chapultepec and Mexico City, winning the rank of brevet captain and a sword of honor from his native state. He was on duty at Fort Laramie, Dakota, when he resigned to enter Confederate service in March 1861. First commissioned major of infantry, he was promoted to brigadier general in the Provisional Army by President Jefferson Davis and given command of the Third Brigade of the Army of the Shenandoah, under General Joseph E. Johnston. His brigade was the first to reinforce Beauregard at Manassas Junction.

Percival Drayton
1812–1865

Drayton, the son of former Congressman William Drayton, began his naval training in 1827 and served in the Brazilian, Mediterranean and Pacific squadrons, the Naval Observatory in Washington and the New York Navy Yard. As part of the South Atlantic Blockading Squadron, Percival Drayton took part in the fall of Port Royal in 1861 and the ironclad boat attack in Charleston Harbor in April 1863; he fought under Farragut at Mobile Bay. In April 1865, Drayton was appointed chief of the Bureau of Navigation in Washington where he became sick and died the following August. A monument was erected in his honor inside Trinity Church in New York City. (In his last days, Drayton added a codicil to his will leaving $30,000 to his brother Thomas who had been impoverished by the war.)

Thomas Fenwick Drayton
1808–1891

Thomas Fenwick Drayton was the brother of Percival Drayton. After his graduation from West Point, he served in the Sixth U.S. Infantry before resigning his commission to run his plantation and work as a railroad director and state legislator. He was commissioned a brigadier general in September 1861 and placed in command of the Port Royal District. He led his brigade at Second Manassas. At South Mountain and Antietam, Drayton's poor performance forced General Lee to reassign him, much to Lee's embarrassment. Drayton spent the last years of the war in the Trans-Mississippi Department. After the war, he farmed in Georgia and then moved to North Carolina where he worked as a life insurance agent. He died in Florence, South Carolina.

WILLIAM HENRY GIST

1807–1874

Gist was born in Charleston, the illegitimate child of Francis Fincher Gist and Mary Boyden. He was recognized by his father and taken to live in the Union district. Upon his father's death, he came under the guardianship of an uncle who petitioned the Charleston District Court of Equity to allow him to bear the Gist family name. Gist studied law at South Carolina College (now the University of South Carolina) and was expelled for boycotting the compulsory boarding regulations. After reading law on his own, he passed the bar and returned to Rose Hill in Union. Gist married and spent four years building a handsome mansion on his plantation. Gist twice ran into difficulties with the law because of his involvement in duels. He served one term in the state house (1844–46) and three in the state senate before being elected South Carolina's sixty-eighth governor. Gist signed the Ordinance of Secession and was a member of the South Carolina Executive Council until it was dissolved in 1862. After the war, Gist took an oath of allegiance and received a pardon from President Andrew Johnson. He returned to Rose Hill, which rapidly declined without slave labor. Rose Hill is now a South Carolina State Historic Site.

ROSE O'NEAL GREENHOW—THE "REBEL ROSE"

1814–1864

Rose Greenhow was a Washington socialite. One of her sisters married Dolly Madison's nephew and another married Stephen A. Douglas. Rose married Dr. Robert Greenhow who worked in the State Department. She became interested in secession politics due to her friendship with John C. Calhoun, and once the war started, she was recruited as a Confederate spy. Greenhow passed information to General P.G.T. Beauregard prior to First Manassas; Jefferson Davis credited this intelligence as a pivotal factor in the Confederate victory. Greenhow was placed under house arrest in August 1861 and was incarcerated in the Old Capitol Prison in January 1862, along with her eight-year-old daughter "Little Rose." In May, she and her daughter were deported to Richmond, where Jefferson Davis enlisted her on diplomatic missions. She was received at the court of Napoleon III in France and had an audience with Queen Victoria. Memoirs about her imprisonment sold briskly in England. Although she became engaged to widowed Lord Granville and had an active social life, Greenhow wanted to aid her friends in the Confederacy. She bought a large supply of women's clothing and took passage on the maiden voyage of the blockade runner *Condor*. Around her neck hung the proceeds of her book, four hundred gold sovereigns. On October 1 during a howling northeaster, *Condor* was discovered and chased by a blockader and ran aground at the mouth of the Cape Fear River. Fearing capture and imprisonment, Greenhow insisted upon going ashore in a rowboat. The little boat capsized in the storm-tossed waters, and weighed down by the heavy pouch suspended from her neck, Greenhow drowned. Her body washed ashore where it was discovered by a young recruit who took the gold. When he learned the identity of the body, he returned it to Colonel William Lamb, commander of Fort Fisher.[98]

JOHNSON HAGOOD
1829–1898

Born in Barnwell, South Carolina, Hagood graduated top of his class at the South Carolina Military Academy (The Citadel). Hagood was admitted to the bar in 1850 but never practiced law. After participating in the defense of Charleston, he returned to Virginia on May 6, 1864, in charge of the First South Carolina Infantry then under General Micah Jenkins, where he served until the surrender of Johnston's forces in April 1865. After the war, he resumed planting. Hagood was elected eightieth governor of South Carolina in 1880. He reopened The Citadel in 1882 and served as chairman of the Board of Visitors until his death in 1898. His book *Memoirs of the War of Secession* was published posthumously in 1910. Built in 1948, The Citadel's football stadium was named in his honor.

JAMES HENRY HAMMOND
1807–1864

Hammond was the sixtieth governor of South Carolina. His father was an ambitious New England laborer who worked his way though Dartmouth College before deciding to seek his fortune in South Carolina. Without either money or social contacts, the elder Hammond eventually became the principal of Mt. Bethel Academy in Newberry. His promising son James Henry attended South Carolina College and mingled with the state's sons of privilege; however, he was keenly aware that he was unable to compete socially. This precipitated debilitating nervous disorders throughout his adulthood.

Hammond published a paper supporting nullification, taught school and practiced law. His ambitions were achieved in 1831 when, over her family's objections, he married a Charleston heiress, Caroline FitzSimons, and took over management of her Silver Hill plantation. Not born to plantation life, he flogged his slaves with his own hand when they transgressed; many died under his care. He served in the U.S. House of Representatives in 1835 until he resigned due to ill health. As governor (1842–44), he converted the South Carolina Arsenal in Charleston into a military academy (The Citadel), conducted a state agricultural survey and urged the legislature to secede rather than accept tariff increases. His political career was tarnished by improper familiarities with four of his wife's nieces, the teenage daughters of Wade Hampton II. The outraged father savaged Hammond's reputation in the state legislature, forcing him to retire from polite society. In 1839, Hammond purchased for his mistress an eighteen-year-old seamstress and her infant daughter. When the daughter was twelve, Hammond took her as a mistress. During his exile, Hammond's wife left him for five years because of his peccadilloes. Hammond died in 1864, leaving behind diaries that intimately described, among other things, "familiarities and dalliances" with the daughters of Wade Hampton II.

Andrew Gordon Magrath

1813–1893

Born in Charleston, Magrath graduated from South Carolina College in 1831 and attended Harvard Law School. He studied law under Judge James L. Petigru and was admitted to the bar in 1835. He served in the state House of Representatives (1838–41). In 1856, Magrath was appointed a Federal judge to the District Court of South Carolina. He sat in the Secession Convention and briefly served as the South Carolina secretary of state. In 1862, he was appointed a Confederate district judge. In December 1864, Magrath was elected seventy-first governor of South Carolina, the last one to be chosen by the state legislature. Governor Magrath was arrested in May 1865 and imprisoned at Fort Pulaski, Georgia. After his release, he returned to Charleston and rebuilt his lucrative law practice. He died in 1893 and was buried in Magnolia Cemetery.

Benjamin Franklin Perry

1805–1886

Perry was born in Pickens District and educated in Ashville, North Carolina. He was admitted to the bar in 1827 but opted to become editor of the *Greenville Mountaineer* in

1832. Opposed to nullification, he became a delegate to both the Union Convention and the Nullification Convention. Emotions ran so high that Perry and Turner Bynum, editor of the pro-Calhoun *Greenville Sentine,* met in a duel in which Perry fatally wounded his opponent. Perry served in both the South Carolina House of Representatives (1836–42, 1849–60) and Senate (1844–48). Although adamantly opposed to secession, Perry rallied Upstate residents to the Confederate cause. Perry was elected to the state house (1862–65) and was appointed a Confederate States District Judge in 1864. Because of his strong Unionist views, President Andrew Johnson appointed Perry provisional governor of South Carolina. Perry led in writing the new state constitution and was elected to the U.S. Senate, although the Radical Republicans in Congress refused to seat him. Perry died in Greenville in 1886.

JAMES LOUIS PETIGRU
1789–1863

James Louis Pettigrew was born in the Abbeville District of South Carolina in 1789 to William and Louise Gibert Pettigrew, daughter of the Reverend Jean Louis Gibert who founded the Huguenot colony of New Bordeaux in 1764; he later changed the spelling of his name to Petigru. He graduated from South Carolina College in 1809 and was admitted to the South Carolina bar in 1812. In 1816, he was elected solicitor of Abbeville County, and in 1822 he became attorney general of South Carolina. In 1830, he was elected to fill a vacant seat in the South Carolina House of Representatives, where he was the leader of the anti-nullificationists. Petigru believed that John C. Calhoun was a very dangerous man and opposed the Confederacy. In 1859, the legislature appointed Judge Petigru to codify South Carolina civil law, a task he finished in 1862. The code was the basis for South Carolina's codification of 1872. Petigru died in Charleston, and despite his strong Unionist views, the whole city closed down to mourn his death. He is buried in St. Michael's Churchyard.

FRANCIS WILKINSON PICKENS
1805–1869

Born in 1805 in Togadoo, St Paul's Parish, Colleton County, Pickens was the son of governor Andrew Pickens and grandson of Revolutionary War hero General Andrew Pickens. Pickens attended Franklin College, Athens, Georgia, and graduated from South Carolina College (now the University of South Carolina). He was admitted to the bar in 1829. A member of the Democratic Party and a supporter of nullification, he served in the state House of Representatives (1832–34) and the U.S. Congress (1834–43). He was a member of the South Carolina senate (1844–46) and was Minister to Russia from 1858 to 1860. Pickens was elected the sixty-ninth governor of South Carolina (1860–62). Although he supported states' rights and secession, he did not sign the Ordinance of Secession. He protested Major Anderson's occupying Fort Sumter and offered to acquire the fort in an equitable settlement of assets. After the war, he was a member of the South Carolina constitutional convention and introduced the motion to repeal the Ordinance of Secession. The motion passed 105–3, with dissenting votes from the Barnwell District. Pickens died in 1869 and was buried in Edgefield.

CHARLES KUHN PRIOLEAU

c. 1840–1887

Prioleau was the son of Judge Samuel Prioleau and Elizabeth Lynch Hamilton. A co-partner in Fraser, Trenholm & Company, he moved to Liverpool and immediately became part of the social scene, becoming an English citizen in 1863. He married renowned beauty Mary Elizabeth Wright who organized several bazaars in St. George's Hall, raising £20,000 for the Southern wounded. Through Fraser, Trenholm & Company, Prioleau financed construction of Confederate navy vessels and purchased arms, artillery and the plates used to print Confederate money. The Confederate government owed Fraser, Trenholm & Company £250,000 when it collapsed. After the war, Prioleau wisely destroyed papers connecting him to the *Alabama* and quietly moved his family to London in 1867 where he disappeared. Prioleau died in 1887 and was buried in Kensal Green Cemetery in London.

ROBERT BARNWELL RHETT

1800–1876

Rhett, né Robert Barnwell Smith, and his brothers changed their surnames to Rhett after their illustrious ancestor, William Rhett, colonial hero who repelled a Spanish flotilla in 1706 and captured the infamous "gentleman pirate," Stede Bonnet. Rhett owned a townhouse in Charleston, two plantations and almost two hundred slaves. He served in the state legislature and was election to Congress in 1837 where he remained until he took Calhoun's seat in the Senate in 1850. Rhett resigned from the Senate in 1852 rather than compromise his secessionist goals. He published the *Charleston Mercury* until his son Robert Barnwell Rhett Jr. became editor in 1857. Rhett Senior settled in Louisiana after the war and died near New Orleans.

MICHAEL USINA

1840–1903

Usina was born in Florida. When he was nineteen, he moved to Savannah, where became an apprentice bar pilot. When the war started, he joined the Oglethorpe Light Infantry, part of the Georgia units that joined General Joseph E. Johnston's army at Harper's Ferry and fought in the Shenandoah Valley. During the heavy fighting at First Manassas, Usina was wounded in the leg. He continued to fight until taken prisoner, but managed to escape. As he could not walk because of his injury, a kindly black man put him on his horse and took him to a Southern camp. After recovering, Usina was assigned to the Confederate navy as pilot in the Savannah Squadron on CSS *Talomico*. Later transferred to blockade running services, he went to England in 1862 to get a masters certificate. By fall, Usina was attached to *Leopard* operated by Trenholm shipping interests. He made runs on *Alice, Douglas (Margaret & Jessie), Flora, Leopard* and *Little Scotia*; he commanded the *Atalanta, Armstrong, Virginia* and *Rattlesnake*, which was deliberately run aground and burned on Sullivan's Island after Fort Fisher fell. Usina ran the blockade into Charleston as a passenger on *Hattie* just before the city surrendered.

$\mathcal{Appendix}$

1864 Runs of the Blockade Runner *Mary Celestia*				
Dates	**Destination**	**Master**	**Chief Engineer**	**Documentation**
May 24–27	St. Georges for Wilmington	Michael Usina	John H. Sassard	Consular dispatch; Wiche, 134, 220; Horner, 103; Vandiver, 131; Wise appendix.
June 2–5	Wilmington for St. Georges	Michael Usina	John H. Sassard	Wiche, 221; Wise appendix.
June 20–24	St. Georges for Wilmington	W.G. Green	John H. Sassard or C.F. Middleton	Wiche, 140; Vandiver, 134; New York Times, July 13, 1864 cites Green as master; Bermuda papers, Usina is listed as master of *Atlanta*; Wise appendix.
June 25–July 3	Wilmington for St. Georges	Michael Usina	John H. Sassard	Cotton tossing, Official Records, War of the Rebellion; Middleton letter July 3; Wise appendix.
July 6–10	St. Georges for Wilmington	Arthur Sinclair	C.F. Middleton	Wiche, 143; Vandiver, 137; Quarantined on arrival until July 24–25. Middleton letter July 8 says Green left and Sinclair his replacement; Wise appendix.
July 25–29	Wilmington for St. Georges	Arthur Sinclair (*NY Times* says W.C. Green)	C.F. Middleton	New York Times Archive, "From the Bermudas: Blockade Runners. Port of Hamilton Arrived. Port of St. George"; Wiche, 147; Middleton letter July 24; Wise appendix.
Aug. 3–7	St. Georges for Wilmington	Arthur Sinclair	C.F. Middleton	Quarantined in NC. Middleton letters dated August 14, 17, 19, 21, 22, 23,25; Vandiver, 138; Middleton letter August 17 says left Bermuda on 3rd arrived at quarantine August 7; Wise appendix.
Aug. 25–30	Wilmington for Hamilton	Arthur Sinclair	C.F. Middleton	Middleton letter August 25 says going to sea that night.
Sept. 6	Hamilton for Wilmington	Arthur Sinclair	C.F. Middleton	*Mary Celestia* sinks—Crew quarantined in Bermuda—Middleton letters dated September 13, 20, 30, 1864; Wise appendix.

Notes

1. Freehling, *Road to Disunion*, 291–317.
2. Alfred Proctor Aldrich (1814–1897) attended the College of Charleston and was admitted to the bar in 1835. He practiced law in Barnwell and was Governor Hammond's confidant during the scandal with Wade Hampton's nieces. Aldrich served five terms in the South Carolina House (1858–65) and was speaker from 1862 to 1865. He was elected judge to the court of pleas and general sessions but was removed from the bench in 1866 by General E.R.S. Canby. Governor Wade Hampton reappointed Aldrich to the court in 1878.
3. Robert Gourdin was forty-eight when he signed the Ordinance of Secession. He was chairman of the Executive Committee of the 1860 Association, and its records are now at Emory University's Manuscript, Archives and Rare Book Library. Gourdin died in 1894 and is buried in Magnolia Cemetery.
4. Freehling, *Road to Disunion*, 385–94.
5. Ibid., 398–400.
6. Porter, *Led On!*, 449–52.
7. Jackson (1820–1898) attended Yale University, served in the Mexican War and went on to become a state judge, the charge d'affaires to the Austrian Empire (1853–54) and minister resident to the Austrian Empire (1854–58). He served in the Confederate army and resumed his law practice after the war. He was minister to Mexico (1885–86) and remained a leader in the business community until his death in 1898.
8. Freehling, *Road to Disunion*, 395–418.
9. *South Carolina Women*, 156.

10. The fervor to secede from the Union was so intense on Edisto Island that its delegate to the Secession Convention, Colonel Joseph Evans Jenkins, passionately thrust his sword into the table and, as the hilt wavered back and forth, declared, "Gentlemen, if South Carolina does not secede from the Union, Edisto Island will." Ironically, Edisto Island was declared indefensible after Union troops captured Port Royal in 1861.

11. *Charleston Mercury*, December 21, 1860.

12. Horton, "Hurlbut Sent as Envoy."

13. Robert Augustus Toombs (1810–1885) was a popular Georgian attorney who served in the Georgia House of Representatives in the 1830s and 1840s. He was elected to the U.S. House of Representatives (1844–53) and went on to the U.S. Senate (1853–61). He was the Confederacy's first secretary of state and later resigned to serve as a Confederate general. After the war, Toombs escaped to Cuba and lived in Europe. He returned via Canada in 1867 and remained an "unreconstructed" Southerner without U.S. citizenship. Toombs was able to restore his lucrative law practice and dominated the Georgia constitutional convention in 1877.

14. *South Carolina Women*, 170–71.

15. Ibid.

16. Gideon Welles (1802–1878) was born in Glastonbury, Connecticut. He was a seventh-generation American whose ancestors immigrated in 1635. Welles participated in politics and was the only man in Connecticut's history to hold all four top offices: governor, deputy governor, treasurer and secretary. He was educated in New England, read law and later transferred to journalism, founding the *Hartford Times* in 1826. He was antislavery and joined the newly formed Republican Party in 1856, where he became a strong supporter of Abraham Lincoln during the presidential election of 1860. He was in Andrew Johnson's cabinet; after the war, he returned to Connecticut where he wrote several books, including *Lincoln and Seward*.

17. Charles Henry Davis (1824–1874) was born in Boston, Massachusetts. He was appointed midshipman in 1824, but because of his intelligence and an education including two years at Harvard, he qualified for a lieutenancy after three years. He worked in the United States Coast Survey researching tides and currents and inspected naval shipyards (1846–49). In 1849, he became superintendent of the Nautical Almanac Office. He was promoted to captain after the fall of Port Royal and later served on the Mississippi River in command of the Western Gunboat Flotilla. He was superintendent of the U.S. Naval Observatory (1865–67) and was one of the founders of the National Academy of Sciences. He authored *The Coast Survey of the United States* and other scientific books.

18. Jones, "The Navy's Stone Fleet."

19. Ibid.

20. Spense, *Confederate Coast*, 142–52, 159–64.

21. Drury, "Civil War's 'Stone Fleet.'"

22. Nepveux, *Trenholm: Financial Genius*, 15–16.

23. Nepveux, *Company that Went to War*, 1–6.

24. Porter, *Led On!*, 112.

25. Nepveux, *Trenholm: Financial Genius*, 58–74.

26. Following the war, neither Bulloch nor his half brother Irvine who sailed on the cruisers *Nashville*, *Alabama* and *Shenandoah* were offered amnesty. Bulloch spent the rest of his life in Liverpool operating a successful business and died January 9, 1901; he was interred in Toxteth Park Cemetery. Bulloch enjoys the distinction of being President Theodore Roosevelt's uncle.

27. Barbet, "When the *Alabama* Struck Her Colors."

28. *Official Records of the Union and Confederate Navies in the War of the Rebellion*, 649–51.

29. Sinclair, *Two Years on the Alabama*, 262.

30. Ibid., 279–81.

31. Brown, "*The Duel Between the Alabama and the Kearsarge*."

32. Vodrey, "The Last Naval Duel."

33. Nepveux, *Company that Went to War*, 97–98.

34. Ibid., 224–29.

35. Cochran, *Blockade Runners*, 331–32.

36. *South Carolina Women*, 161–63.

37. Boaz and Nepveux, "Dashing Blockade Runner."

38. Michael, *Lelia*, 15–23, 32–33, 41–42, 142–49.

39. Captain Crenshaw's wife and children ran the blockade to join him in England. Because of the severe recriminations of the Radical Republicans after the war, the family remained abroad until 1868. Louis D. Crenshaw and his daughters arrived in England in January 1866 and James Crenshaw joined the family shortly thereafter. Captain Crenshaw was more fortunate than most. Hard work and business ability enabled him to recoup financially through the fertilizer industry; he died a wealthy man in 1897.

40. The 103-foot half-brig *Mary Celeste* was launched in Nova Scotia in 1860. After several accidents, she was put up for a salvage auction. Repaired and renamed *Mary Celeste*, she left New York under Captain Benjamin Briggs, who was accompanied by his wife, young daughter and a crew of eight. *Mary Celeste*'s passengers were never seen again. The drifting derelict was discovered and investigated by a British Board of Inquiry, which ruled out piracy or foul play. Arthur Conan Doyle, writing under a pseudonym, later fictionalized the incident in "J. Habakuk Jepson's Statement."

41. Walter George Green was born in Liverpool in 1827 and received his master's certificate in 1861 at Glasgow. He commanded the steamer *Souchays* and *Red Jacket* (alias of the blockade runner *Dundroon Castle*) until it ran onto a reef on October 11, 1863. His next command was *Mary Celestia*. The steamer's maiden voyage took her to Bermuda via the Azores in May 1864. She was reported as "*Mary Collert*" in a consular dispatch from São Miguel in the Azores on May 9. Consular Agent Thomas Hickling reported May 3, "The (two-masted and two-funnel) schooner *Mary Collert* [sic] 248 tons, Captain W.G. Green, arrived from Liverpool, bound to Nassau for coal, and departed with upwards of 200 tons. She had the appearance of being destined for a Confederate cruiser; the master said she can steam 18 miles an hour." In a separate dispatch, Hickling noted that the English steamer *Mary Celestina*, from Glasgow for Bermuda, took in coal in the Azores on May 3. *Mary Celestia* arrived at Bermuda on May 16. The U.S. consul in Bermuda, Charles Maxwell Allen, noted in his May 20 dispatch, "The British steamer *Mary Celestia* from London or Liverpool arrived here on the 17th [sic], side wheel, two stacks fore and aft, two masts, about 250 tons, is now painted white, and taking in cargo." Ten days later, he reported "The following steamers have left here to run the blockade, probably for Wilmington…May 24. *Mary Celestia*, Usina, Master." Provided by James Delgado, College of Charleston Special Collections Library, Eastman collection, Charleston, South Carolina.

42. Records vary on whether he was captain of *Mary Celestia* on three or four runs. See Appendix.

43. John H. Sassard was a member of Trinity Church and died of heart disease in 1883.

44. Talk to Confederate Veterans Association of Savannah, July 4, 1893.

45. McNeil, *Pilots of the Mary Celestia*, Chapter 4. According to James Delgado, Union records are silent on any firing on or chasing an inbound steamer on that date. Two days later, they reported shooting at and chasing someone leaving Wilmington. (College of Charleston Special Collections Library, Eastman collection, Charleston, South Carolina.)

46. *The War of the Rebellion*, 42.

47. Courtesy James Delgado, College of Charleston Special Collections Library, Eastman collection, Charleston, South Carolina.

48. Michael, *Lelia*, 45.

49. Due to conflicting reports after the shipwreck, the exact number of men aboard will be forever shrouded in mystery. According to Steven Brown's article, published in the *Confederate Veteran* magazine 2 (1995) on January 13, 1865, three firemen and one seaman obtained permission to go ashore. They failed to arrive before *Lelia* set sail with forty-five [forty-six] aboard. According to Chris Michael,

the Board of Trade Inquiry is reported in two Liverpool newspapers: *Mercury* and *Courier*. Michael stipulated in his Appendix that the versions are in disagreement and quoted both (using brackets).

50. Michael, *Lelia*, 71–76.

51. His obituary stated that his involvement in the building of blockade runners was a matter of business and not from any sympathy with the Confederates. The Alabama Claims between the United States and Britain had not been settled, and the newspaper that reported his death did not wish to appear inflammatory. It was Miller who recommended his son-in-law, James Alexander Duguid, to Bulloch as a captain for *Oreto* (later *Florida*). Miller was an acquaintance of William Gladstone, later Britain's prime minister. Because of the importance of cotton to the port of Liverpool and the Lancashire cotton mills, many politicians in Britain favored an early end to the conflict to relieve the economic distress in the mill towns. In a speech on October 7, 1862, Gladstone had argued that the leaders of the South had "made an army, they are making, it appears, a navy; and, they have made what is more than either, a nation." Many viewed this speech as impending recognition of the Confederacy. Miller, like Gladstone, was a member of the Liberal Party and had once loaned Gladstone the use of an office during one of his election campaigns. Courtesy Richard Harris, a direct descendant of W.C. Miller, College of Charleston Special Collections Library, Eastman collection , Charleston, South Carolina.

52. Eastman, *Remembering Old Charleston*, 53–64.

53. Elson, "Secrets of the Deepdeep."

54. Phelps, *Charlestonians in War*, 17–23.

55. Benjamin A. Johnson was educated at Williamsburg, Virginia. He studied law with Colonel DeTreville and practiced in Beaufort. In 1838, he was elected to the House of Representatives from St. Helena Parish, where he served until he was transferred to the Senate, serving two terms. During his residence in Beaufort, he commanded the Twelfth Regiment of Infantry. When he moved to Christ Church Parish, he became a member of the state House of Representatives from that district. He was forty-five at the time of his death. Obituary, *Charleston Mercury*.

56. Rosen, *Confederate Charleston*, 83; Flannagan, "The Big Gun Shoot."

57. Flannagan, "The Big Gun Shoot."

58. Rosen, *Confederate Charleston*, 89.

59. Giles, "A Hurricane of Fire."

60. *South Carolina Women*, 172–73.

61. Phelps, *Charlestonians in War*, 43–44.

62. Giles, "A Hurricane of Fire."

63. Ibid.

64. Hagood, *Memoirs of the War*, 208.

65. Phelps, *Charlestonians in War*, 45–53.

66. Smalls's escape gave him celebrity in the North and was part of the basis for permitting African Americans to serve in the Union army. Congress awarded prize money for the capture of *Planter* to Smalls and the crewmen. Smalls was appointed captain of *Planter* by an army contract in 1863; he returned to Charleston harbor in April 1865 for the re-raising of the American flag upon Fort Sumter. After the war, Smalls returned to Beaufort and purchased his former master's house at a tax sale. During Reconstruction, he became a Republican state legislator and served five terms in the U.S. Congress.

67. Behre, "Daring Voyage to Freedom."

68. Hamilton, "Battle of Secessionville"; Simonowicz, "Fort Lamar, James Island."

69. Called a "lawyer of high culture" by General Johnson Hagood, Ramsey was educated both in America and at the University of Heidelberg. His maternal grandfather was Henry Laurens, president of the Continental Congress, who was imprisoned in the Tower of London and exchanged for Lord Cornwallis after his surrender at Yorktown. His paternal grandfather was historian Dr. David Ramsey, a colonial doctor who brought the smallpox vaccination to the South, served as a surgeon in the Revolution and was imprisoned in St. Augustine for eleven months during the British occupation of Charles Town.

70. Hendricks's ancestors were Dutch adventurers who came with Hendrik Hudson in the early seventeenth century. The Hendricks family fought with Francis Marion's partisans at King's Mountain, Camden, Cowpens and Charles Town. Henry Hendricks's father lacked the means to raise his children and placed two sons in the Charleston Orphan House on February 23, 1833. Young Hendricks was bound out to the U.S. Naval School and trained on the USS *Cyane* in the Pacific Station from 1841 to 1844. He was thirty-five when he joined the Charleston Battalion in 1861; he was later promoted to second lieutenant in Colonel P.C. Gaillard's regiment.

71. Phelps, *Charlestonians in War*, 96.

72. Power, "Brother Against Brother."

73. Phelps, *Charlestonians in War*, 135.

74. Emilio, *A Brave Black Regiment*, 98.

75. *New York Times*, "Read the Union Signals."

76. Wise, *Gate of Hell*, 148–50; McClure, *Annals of the Civil War*, 95–110.

77. Davis, "Siege of Morris Island."

78. Bordewich, "A Civil Battle."

79. Phelps, *Charlestonians in War*, 145–49.

NOTES TO PAGES 125–174

80. www.27th-scvi.org/history.htm.

81. Waring, "Fort Sumter Hero."

82. Phelps, *Charlestonians in War*, 153–77.

83. Ibid., 187–88.

84. Ibid., 189–90.

85. Trott Family papers, College of Charleston Special Collections Library, Charleston, South Carolina.

86. Ibid.

87. *Confederate Home and College*, 5–12; Phillips, *City of the Silent*, 160–61; Margaret Simons Middleton, College of Charleston Special Collections Library, Eastman collection, Charleston, South Carolina.

88. Sarna, *Jews and the Civil War*, 161.

89. Phillips, "Journal of Mrs. Eugenia Levy Phillips, 1861–1862."

90. Sarna, *Jews and the Civil War*, 267–76; "Journal of Mrs. Eugenia Phillips."

91. Meskauskas, *Civil War Times*.

92. Pember, *A Southern Woman's Story*, 33.

93. Ibid., 33.

94. Ibid., 85–86.

95. Sarna, *Jews and the Civil War*, 288-291.

96. Clary, *Evacuation of Confederate Forces*.

97. *South Carolina Women*, 164–68.

98. Horner, *The Blockade Runners*, 34–62; Cochran, *Blockade Runners of the Confederacy*, 133–41.

Bibliography

Anderson, Dorothy Middleton. "Family Letters of My Great Grandfather." *Bermuda Historical Quarterly* 28, no. 4.

Barbet, Paul. "When The Alabama Struck Her Colors, Captain Semmes Tells of Battle With the Kearsarge." *Richmond Times Dispatch*, circa 1936.

Behre, Robert. "A Daring Voyage to Freedom." *Charleston (SC) Post and Courier*, January 2, 2012.

Bleser, Carol, ed. *Secret and Sacred, The Diaries of James Henry Hammond, a Southern Slaveholder.* New York: Oxford University Press, 1988.

Boaz, Thomas M., and Ethel Trenholm Seabrook Nepveux. "Dashing Blockade Runner: Captain Thomas J. Lockwood." *Military Images*, May/June.

Bordewich, Fergus M. "A Civil Battle for a Civil War Battlefield." *Smithsonian Magazine*, July 2005.

Browne, John M. "The Duel Between the *Alabama* and the *Kearsarge*." http://www.civilwarhome.com/duel.htm.

Charleston Mercury. May 19, 1863.

Clary, James B. *Evacuation of Confederate Forces from Charleston in 1865, A History of the 15th South Carolina Volunteer Infantry: 1861-65.* http://ehistory.osu.edu/uscw/features/regimental/south_carolina/confederate/KershawsBrigade/15th.cfm.

Cochran, Hamilton. *Blockade Runners of the Confederacy.* New York: Bobbs-Merrill Company, Inc., 1958.

Crenshaw, William G., III. "Captain William G. Crenshaw, C.S.A. The War Years." Richmond: Virginia State Library, 1960.

Davis, W.W.H. "The Siege of Morris Island," From *Annals of the Civil War Written by Leading Participants North and South.* Alexander Kelly McClure, ed. Reprint, New York: DaCapo Press, 1994.

Drury, David. "Civil War's 'Stone Fleet' Sailed From New London To Dubious End In South Carolina." *Hartford Courant*, December 10, 2011.

Eastman, Margaret Middleton Rivers. *Remembering Old Charleston, A Peek Behind Parlor Doors.* Charleston, SC: The History Press, 2008

Eastman, Margaret Middleton Rivers, and Edward Fitzsimons Good. *Hidden History of Old Charleston*. Charleston, SC: The History Press, 2010.

Elson, Peter. "Secrets of the Deepdeep: The Discovery of an Internationally Important Shipwreck in Liverpool Bay is Told in a New Book and Will Be Featured on Television This Week." *Daily Post*, August 25, 2004.

Emilio, Luis F. *A Brave Black Regiment: The History of the Fifty-fourth Regiment of Massachusetts Volunteer Infantry, 1863–65*. New York: Da Capo Press, 1995.

Flannagan, Roy. "The Big Gun Shoot of November 7, 1861: The Battle for Port Royal Sound." (South Carolina Historical Society) *Carologue*, Winter 2011.

Freehling, William W. *The Road to Disunion, Volume II Secessionists Triumphant 1854–1861*. New York: Oxford University Press, 200?

Giles, Katherine W. "A Hurricane of Fire   at Charleston Fire of 1861." (South Carolina Historical Society) *Carologue*,   1.

Hagood, Johnson. *Memoirs of the War of ?   ?mbia, SC: State Company, 1910.

Hamilton, William J., III. "The Battle o   ?e." www.civilwar.org/battlefields/secessionville/secessionville-history-?

*Historical Sketch of the Confederate Home   ?arleston, SC: Walker, Evans & Cogswell, 1921.

Horner, Dave. *The Blockade Runners*. N?   ?lead & Company, 1968.

Horton, Tom. "Hurlbut sent as envo?   ? 1861." *Charleston (SC) Moultrie News*, April 5, 2011.

Jones, Jamie L. "The Navy's Stone Fl?   ?, January 26, 2012.

Ladies Calhoun Monument Associat?   ? *Calhoun Monument at Charleston, S.C.* Charleston, SC: Lucas, Richa?   ?888.

McNeil, Jim. *Masters of the Shoals: Cap?   ?he Union Blockade*. Cambridge, MA: DaCapo Press, 2003.

Meskauskas, Mary C. *Civil War Times?   ?torynet.com.

Michael, Chris. *Lelia*. Liverpool, Eng?   ?cation, Liverpool Marine Press, 2004.

Nepveux, Ethel S. *George Alfred Trenholm?   ?ent to War*. Anderson, SC: Electric City Printing Company, 199?

———. *George A. Trenholm: Financial Geni?   ?deracy*. Anderson, SC: Electric City Printing Company, 1999.

New York Times. "The Bombardment and Evacuation of Forts Wagner and Gregg." September 15, 1863.

———. "Read the Union Signals, Mr. Lowndes Valuable Services to the Confederacy." July 31, 1892.

Official Records of the Union and Confederate Navies in the War of the Rebellion. Series 1, vol. 3. Washington, D.C.: Government Printing Office, 1896.

Owens, Jody, *Philip Usina "The Boy Captain."* Vol. 13 *Savannah Biographies*. Savannah, GA: Lane Library, Armstrong Atlantic State University, 1985.

Pember, Phoebe Yates. *A Southern Woman's Story*. Columbia: University of South Carolina Press, 2002.

Phelps, W. Chris. *Charlestonians In War*. Gretna, LA: Pelican Publishing Company, 2004.

Phillips, Eugenia Levy. "Journal of Mrs. Eugenia Levy Phillips, 1861–1862." *Memoirs of American Jews, 1776-1865* 3, Jewish Publication Society, 1955, vol. 3, p.161. Original papers at the Library of Congress.

Phillips, Ted Ashton, Jr. *City of the Silent*. Columbia: University of South Carolina Press, 2010.

Porter, A. Toomer. *Led On! Step by Step*. New York: Arno Press, 1967.

Power, J. Tracey. "Brother Against Brother: Alexander and James Campbell's Civil War." *South Carolina Historical Magazine* (April 1994).

Rosen, Robert N. *Confederate Charleston, An Illustrated History of the City and the People During the Civil War*. Columbia: University of South Carolina Press, 1994.

Sarna, Jonathan D., and Adam Mendlesohn. *Jews and the Civil War*. New York University Press, 2010.

Scott, W.W. "Biography of Captain William G. Crenshaw." in *A History of Orange County, Virginia*. Richmond, VA: Everett Waddy & Company, 1907.

Sebrell, Thomas E. "The Charleston-Liverpool Civil War Connection." *Charleston Mercury*, September 22, 2009.

Simonowicz, Vincent J., III. "Fort Lamar, James Island, SC, Scene of the Battle of Secessionville June 1861." www.csa-sca-scla.org/articles/fort_Lamar.htm.

Sinclair, Arthur. *Two Years on the Alabama*. Boston: Lee and Shepard, 1896.

Spense, E. Lee. *Treasures of the Confederate Coast: "The Real Rhett Butler: and Other Revelations."* Miami/Charleston: Narwhal Press, 1995.

United Daughters of the Confederacy, South Carolina Division, *South Carolina Women in the Confederacy, Vol I*. Columbia, SC: State Company, 1903.

Vandiver, Frank E. *Confederate Blockade Running Through Bermuda 1861–1865; Letters and Cargo Manifests*. Austin: University of Texas Press, 1947.

Vodrey, William F.B. "The Last Naval Duel: The USS *Kearsarge* v the CSS *Alabama*," Civil War Roundtable. Bucyrus, Ohio, March 2002.

Waring, Tom. "Fort Sumter Hero Begins Family Military Tradition." *Charleston (SC) News and Courier*, August 19, 1979.

The War of the Rebellion, A Compilation of the Official Records of the Union and Confederate Armies, Series I-volume I. Washington, D.C.: Government Printing Office, 1880.

Wiche, Glen N., ed. *Dispatches from Bermuda: The Civil War Letters of Charles Maxwell Allen, United States Consul at Bermuda, 1861–1888*. Kent, OH: Kent State University Press, 2008.

Wise, Stephen R. *Gate of Hell, Campaign for Charleston Harbor, 1863*. Columbia: University of South Carolina Press, 1994.

———. *Lifeline of the Confederacy*. Appendices 5 and 6. Columbia: University of South Carolina Press, 1991.

www.27th-sevi.org/history.htm.

About the Author

Margaret M.R. Eastman, known to her friends as Peg, is a Charleston native whose family dates back to the early settlers of the Carolina colony. She is interested in history and continues to promote Charleston's rich cultural heritage through her writings. After her marriage, she moved away and was a professional guide at Winterthur Museum in Delaware. Locally, she has lectured on certain characteristic elements of Charleston architecture and is actively involved with the Preservation Society's Master Conservation program. She worked for a time in resources development at the American College of the Building Arts.

Photograph by Cheryl Paul.

Peg Eastman is a freelance writer for the *Charleston Mercury*, and during her consulting career in job documentation, co-authored with James R. Sawers *Certifying Workers Skills in the Chemical Industry*, published by McGraw-Hill. She edited and published her mother's poems *Verses by Marwee* (2004). Through The History Press, she co-authored with her brother *Mendel and Me, Life with Congressman L. Mendel Rivers (The Serviceman's Best Friend)* and recently released *Old Charleston Originals from Celebrities to Scoundrels* (2011). *Remembering Old Charleston: A Peek Behind Parlor Doors* (2008) and *Hidden History of Old Charleston* (2010), co-authored with Edward Good, are both enjoying a fourth printing.

On a personal note, she belongs to St. Michael's Church and is a member of several local organizations and national societies. She has two sons and two grandsons.